Miracle on the Mountain
and other true missionary stories

BRADLEY BOOTH

Pacific Press® Publishing Association
Nampa, Idaho
Oshawa, Ontario, Canada
www.pacificpress.com

Cover design by Gerald Lee Monks
Cover design resources from Dreamstime.com
Inside design by Kristin Hansen-Mellish

The author assumes full responsibility for the accuracy of all facts and quotations as cited in this book.

Scriptures marked KJV are from the King James Version.

Scriptures marked NIV are from THE HOLY BIBLE, NEW INTERNATIONAL VERSION®, NIV® copyright © 1973, 1978, 1984, 2011 by Biblica, Inc.™ Used by permission. All rights reserved worldwide.

Scriptures marked NKJV are from The New King James Version, copyright © 1979, 1980, 1982, Thomas Nelson, Inc., Publishers.

Additional copies of this book may be obtained by calling toll-free 1-800-765-6955 or online at http://www.adventistbookcenter.com.

ISBN 13: 978-0-8163-4106-1
ISBN 10: 0-8163-4106-0

12 13 14 15 16 • 5 4 3 2 1

Dedication

This book is dedicated to the Seventh-day Adventist missionaries of yesteryear, who stepped out in faith and took the gospel to the world. Across the globe, they sacrificed much for Jesus that others might hear the three angels' messages. May God inspire us today to follow their example and spread the good news of Jesus' soon coming.

Contents

Miracle on the Mountain

Part 1: "God Will Help You Find a Way" — 7
Part 2: Trek to Surabaya — 10
Part 3: The Mudflow Parted — 13

In Harm's Way

Part 1: Drafted — 17
Part 2: "Just Shoot the Gun!" — 20
Part 3: Locked in the "Hole" — 22
Part 4: Back in the "Hole" — 25
Part 5: Charged With Insubordination — 28
Part 6: Acquitted of All Charges — 30

A Second Day of Pentecost

Part 1: Ioana's Surprise — 33
Part 2: Why All the Chairs? — 36
Part 3: "They Think You Speak Romanian" — 39

Military Missionaries

Part 1: Victims of a Purge — 43
Part 2: Genya's Study Group — 45
Part 3: "Can You Baptize Us?" — 47
Part 4: The Mayor Sides With the Adventists — 50

Create in Me a Clean Heart

Part 1: Flee on the Evening Train — 53
Part 2: "We Know All About You Advents" — 56
Part 3: "The Guards'll Be Coming for You Soon" — 58
Part 4: "You Must Buy Her" — 61

Rain Man

Part 1: Finding a Meeting Place — 65

Part 2: The Miraculous Rainstorm — 68

Missionary Journey

Part 1: Paralyzed by the Witch Doctor — 73

Part 2: Women's Prayers Answered — 76

Part 3: Finding Sabbath Keepers at Last — 78

Part 4: Paralytic to Evangelist — 81

Kiss the Ring

Part 1: The Mayor Frees Akim — 85

Part 2: Cosmina Speaks Up — 88

Never Too Old

Part 1: Send Me — 91

Part 2: Exhausting Voyage — 93

Part 3: "Can You R-R-Read It for Me?" — 95

Wings of a Dove

Part 1: Dakila's Dream — 99

Part 2: New Sabbath Congregation in Natonin — 102

Impossible Dream

Part 1: "I Dreamed I Saw Those Guys!" — 107

Part 2: "You Must Be Messengers From God" — 110

Miracle Catch

Part 1: American Missionary Arrives in Pakhoi — 115

Part 2: The First Sabbath Keepers — 118

Part 3: A Storm Like a Monster — 121

Part 4: Hunger, Illness, and Debt — 123

Part 5: Faith Restored, Miracle Follows — 125

Miracle on the Mountain

Part 1: "God Will Help You Find a Way"

In a little mountain village on the island of Java there once lived an old Chinese woman. Li Hua was shy, as women of that culture often tended to be, but proud of the cultural heritage from which she had descended. Everyone knew her to be a good woman, always kind and always willing to lend a hand to her neighbors in times of need.

She had become a Seventh-day Adventist a few years earlier, when a traveling colporteur had come through and shared the story of the gospel with her. But there were no other Adventists in her village and, in those early years of mission work, no pastor who could come to visit her from time to time.

Li Hua earned a living by growing vegetables on the rich volcanic soil of the mountain and then selling them in the local markets. She didn't have to go far, for there were always people who wished to buy the sweet potatoes and squash she raised in her little plot of ground.

The mountain was an old volcano. Though it had been known to erupt in the distant past—spewing fire and ash and hot lava down its slopes—for now it seemed to content itself with low rumbles and light tremors from time to time. No one took the old mountain seriously. After all, folks had been living on its slopes for generations, and no one had ever seen the mountain do more than puff a few wisps of gray-blue smoke.

When Li Hua became an Adventist Christian, she learned many things from the Bible. Chen Ru, the traveling colporteur, told her stories about God the Creator, how He had made the world in six days and then rested on the seventh. He shared with her the miracles that God had performed for His people, such as the parting of the Red Sea, raining manna from heaven, and providing water from the rock. He told her that Jesus had come to live in this world and that He died on a cruel cross to pay for our sins.

Li Hua was touched by these stories and the love of a God who would do so much to save a world lost in sin. The religion of her people was nothing like this. A peace settled in her heart when she listened to Chen Ru and discovered that God cared about her personally. Tears welled up in her eyes as she realized that God would hear her and help her if she called on Him in prayer.

When Chen Ru told her about the seventh-day Sabbath and that Christians should not do any work on God's holy day, she gladly accepted this Bible teaching. How could she refuse this request by God, who had given His life for her?

The Christian gospel was truly good news for a hardworking old woman, and the Sabbath now became a very important part of her spiritual life. Each Saturday found her in her house, singing praises to God in her sweet, quavering voice. There were no other believers to worship with her, but she did her best to remember the Bible verses Chen Ru had taught her. She couldn't read and had no Bible, so she simply quoted the Bible verses from memory as best as she could.

But it was her prayer time that was most special. Each time Li Hua bowed on her knees to her heavenly Father, it seemed that Heaven drew very near. And indeed it did, for when the old woman went outside at the end of the day, the villagers could see the peace of God on her angelic face.

Li Hua did what she could to be a witness to the other villagers, telling them of the love she had for her heavenly Father; but they avoided her. She was just too different. The changes in her since she had become a Christian had put a gulf between them. She no longer drank the musty beer they made from sweet brown molasses. And strangest of all, she no longer worshiped the spirits and traditional idols of the village ancestors at the shrines.

The villagers lived in fear of the spirits and the evil they could bring. Jiang, the local witch doctor, seemed to be the only buffer between his people and the spirit world. His advice was sought, and his words revered—but only because the villagers feared the spirit world so much. Often he brought more harm than help to their superstitious lives.

The amulets and fetishes and chicken bones Jiang carried around with him in a dirty leather bag were more than just good-luck charms. They were the tools of his trade, used to forecast the weather, treat sickness, and tell young couples when to marry. No one could make a move, it was believed, without consulting the witch doctor. To do so invited the worst sort of trouble.

When children with stomachaches were carried into his hut on bamboo litters, he said the evil spirits were inside of them, trying to get out. Not surprisingly, the potions of ginger root and bat's blood and lizard tail that he forced them to drink made them even sicker.

If a leopard on the prowl stole a pig from the village herd, someone was to blame for making the spirits angry. The owner of the missing pig was usually considered the culprit, and Jiang would promptly banish him from the village for a fortnight.

If the rains didn't come to water the gardens, the villagers were to blame for not offering enough rice and incense at the shrines.

"How can you refuse to worship the spirits?" the villagers would demand. "Don't you remember the power they have over us, Li Hua?"

But the little old woman no longer feared the spirits or the ugly little stone shapes that represented the spirits of the jungle. "They cannot hurt me," she told the villagers bravely. "God can protect me from them and all they would do to harm me."

"But if you reject them for this new God of yours, the spirits will be angry with us!" The villages glared at her fearfully.

"Then I will pray for you," Li Hua promised respectfully. "I am so happy worshiping my great God, and I wish you could know Him as I do."

"You're a crazy old woman!" the villagers would retort. "We will never give up honoring the spirits! We will never worship your God!"

Chen Ru had showed Li Hua in the Bible that idols made by human beings are nothing more than wood and stone. "The village folks can offer the idols gifts of food and molasses beer and incense," he said, "but the idols have no eyes, so they cannot see. They have no ears, so they cannot hear the people's prayers. They have no mouths, so they cannot speak or taste the simple offerings the villagers give them. But the Father in heaven can see us and hear us, and He can speak to our hearts when we need Him most."

And other things made Li Hua different too. Chen Ru had taught her that one-tenth of all she earned belonged to God. Every blessing she received in life was from God, he told her. Her health, her happiness, the air she breathed, even the meager income she received from selling the vegetables she grew—they were blessings from God. Chen Ru had explained that because God owned everything, she should pay a faithful tithe on everything He blessed her with as income.

With her knowledge of God and the life of peace and hope He had given her, Li Hua was a new person now. She would gladly do what God asked, but there was one problem. Without a church or pastor, to whom would she give her tithe?

Chen Ru thought about that for a moment. "Well, Grandma," he said, using the affectionate name with which he addressed her whenever they talked, "I suppose you could send it from time to time with someone who goes down to the city. You could have them take it to the mission in Surabaya."

Li Hua raised her eyebrows doubtfully. "I would rather not do that," she said slowly. "I do not think I can trust anyone from this village with God's money."

"Well, don't worry about it then," Chen Ru assured her. "God will help you find a way." And he patted her shoulder reassuringly.

Li Hua thought about her problem after Chen Ru left and finally decided she must come up with her own solution. She would make the journey herself from the mountain to the coastal city of Surabaya to pay her tithe. It was a bold decision, for the journey was long, and the way was dangerous. Wild pigs and poisonous snakes and insects inhabited the forest, but there seemed no other way. She was determined to be faithful in paying her tithes to God, and the mission was the only place she knew of where she could do that. She didn't have much to give, but the few coppers she had been saving spoke volumes about her loyalty to God and her church.

Part 2: Trek to Surabaya

Li Hua headed north early one morning at sunrise, hobbling out of the village and down the jungle trail. "Guide my steps to the mission station, Lord," she prayed as she descended the steep mountain, gingerly picking her way over the tree roots and boulders in her way. "I will depend on You completely, for You are my Shield and Protector."

By noon she had reached the base of the mountain, and now began the hardest part of her journey. The jungle trail was plain to see, but here and there across the pathway hung branches and vines. She did not carry a machete with her, and she would not have had strength enough to swing it anyway. Now and then, she had to climb over a fallen log or get down on her hands and knees to crawl under it, if it was high enough above the ground.

When she came to streams, she had to wade across, stopping only long enough to get a drink. About midafternoon, she stopped to rest and eat a boiled sweet potato and bathe her tired feet in cool water. And then it was up and on the trail again to cover as many miles as she could before darkness descended on the jungle.

A few times, she met people coming her way up the trail, and always she greeted them with a smile. She did not recognize any of them, but the jungle trail was a lonely place for a little old woman, making any face a welcome sight.

On she walked, her feet growing sore from the rough pathway. Her joints ached from a small shoulder pack and sleeping mat she had strapped to her back, but she pushed on.

By nightfall, she was worn out. The foliage of the jungle canopy was thick, but here and there she could see that the sky above had turned a darker blue. Darkness was coming fast—dusk waits for no one near the equator. In a matter of minutes, the blackness of night would be her enemy.

Li Hua hurried to prepare a little campsite. First, she must gather the wood she needed for a fire; and though she needed only a few sticks for cooking, she must also have a good supply to keep the wild animals away. Once she had a fire going, she set a little pot of tea on the coals, and then sharpened a pointed stick and propped it over the fire to cook a sweet potato.

Darkness had come now, but still she worried there wasn't enough wood. She knew the jungle was no place to be without a good fire at night, so she scouted along the trail in the flickering shadows of the fire and found a few more sticks. Only then did she allow herself to squat on her heels and rest by the fire's cheery glow.

Before eating, she thanked the Lord for His care along the jungle trail and for the simple food she would eat. She hardly had the strength, it seemed, to sip the warm tea and chew the blackened sweet potato on the stick, but she was so hungry that the food tasted delicious.

When she finished, she cleared a spot on the ground near the fire and spread out her sleeping mat. As she lay down and closed her eyes, she sent another prayer heavenward, asking God to care for her through the long night; and then she slept.

It was the sweet sleep of fatigue; and the next thing she knew, dawn was brightening the morning sky above. Strangely enough, her body felt rested and her joints no longer ached as they had the day before. "Thank You, Lord," she prayed as she heated herself a bit of tea. Rolling up her mat, she tied it and the pack on her back before heading down the trail.

Eventually, the terrain leveled out, and it was easier to walk the jungle trails. Now she made better time. Her journey continued until she could see the spires of Surabaya's Buddhist temple through the trees. When she emerged from the jungle, she asked for directions to the Seventh-day Adventist mission and had no trouble finding it. Everybody seemed to know where it was.

At the gate to the mission compound, she asked for a pastor and was sent to the mission director. As she stood before him telling him her story, he marveled at her determination to make the long trek from the mountain, and at her faith that God would bring her safely to the city. She produced the small bag of coppers from her shoulder pack and placed it carefully in his hands, closing his fingers around the bag as if he were holding something precious.

And truly he was, for he understood the monumental effort it had taken her to get these coins to the city. To some, it might seem an ordinary thing she had done, but to him it was an extraordinary accomplishment.

In reverence he bowed his head to pray with her and thank God for her tithe and her faithfulness.

Then the mission director invited Li Hua to eat the evening meal with him and his wife, and to stay the night as a guest. She smiled shyly as she ate the simple meal of rice served with *paku,* a jungle fern. She thanked the mission director for his kindness and then rolled out her little sleeping mat on the floor of the room they offered her.

Before she lay down, she knelt and thanked God once again for His care and her safe arrival at the mission. Without a doubt, the angels of heaven had guarded her steps and kept the evil one from harming her.

Not surprisingly, she slept soundly that night, but she was up again at the crack of dawn to eat a quick meal and be on her way. Before daylight had stretched its amber fingers over the ocean, she was gone, back again the way she had come with her little steps on that rugged jungle trail.

The months passed; and then about six months later, Li Hua showed up at the mission station again, bringing with her the treasured offering of coppers she had saved for the Lord. The little coins she emptied into the mission director's hands were a pittance indeed, but once again the effort they represented was colossal. As before, she had saved her tithe from the sale of garden produce, and here she was turning it over to the Lord to be used to help spread the gospel.

The mission director celebrated her arrival again with a warm evening meal, and this time others came to share in the moment. Truly, Li Hua was an inspiration to them all of what simple faith and determination can do for a Christian. Not surprisingly, Li Hua did not stay long at the mission. The next morning she was off again at dawn to begin the long trip home.

The journey was a long and trying ordeal for a woman her age, but it was her testimony to those who were watching. She must pay her tithe. What better way to show her love for Jesus who had given His life for her.

When she came yet again six months later, everyone at the mission station was called together, and they all crowded around to greet her. Now they began to realize just how important this trek of hers had become for them all, how symbolic and meaningful for each of them in their walk with God.

In the months and years that followed, her treks became a regular part of the mission calendar, something the missionaries all found themselves looking forward to with joyful anticipation.

"My God shall supply all my need," she always told the mission group when they asked how she managed things for herself up on the rugged mountain. She had to tend a garden and live in a village that was not at all friendly, and she had to do it alone with no relatives or fellow church members to help her. And then she made the strenuous journey to the city to deliver her precious tithe twice a year. Truly, the missionaries found themselves encouraged and heartened by Li Hua's life of sacrificial giving.

And then one day in 1919, the mountain above Li Hua's village began rumbling again. Some in the village glanced up at the misty peak, but most ignored it. They were used to hearing the old volcano growl. They had grown accustomed to seeing it huff and puff its clouds of smoke.

But suddenly one morning soon after, the mountain erupted with a terrific roar and a deafening explosion. The blast sent shockwaves across the mountain peak and into the surrounding valley. Smoke and ash showered everywhere, blocking out the sun, pelting the local villagers, and making it hard to breathe. But worse was to come.

The mountain's eruption produced *lahars*—huge flows of mud that became as hard as concrete when the flows stopped. These rivers of mud poured down the mountain's steep slopes, destroying everything in their path. Like avalanches, they swallowed mountain streams, wiped out fleeing animals, and flattened sections of forest. Many small villages were inundated by the *lahars,* and at least five thousand people perished. It was truly a frightening sight, even for the people living far away in the coastal cities to the north.

Part 3: The Mudflow Parted

The missionaries at the station in Surabaya watched in horror as the volcano's destruction continued. They prayed for the villages they were sure must be in the path of the flowing debris, and asked that the heavenly Father minimize the damage. There was little else they could do. Many of the folks living on the slopes of the mountain had never heard the gospel story, and the missionaries' hearts went out in sympathy to those who would surely die from this dreadful disaster.

Hours passed as a dense pillar of smoke engulfed the spouting volcano. Reports coming in told of horrific damage up on the mountain with entire villages buried beneath *lahars.*

Then someone had a thought of the elderly Chinese woman who lived up on the mountain. Li Hua—what had become of her? Had she escaped from the fiery inferno, or had she perished with the thousands of other villagers who never made it to safety? Would they ever see her again? The chances of survival for a woman her age seemed slim indeed.

Months passed and then someone noticed the calendar. It was the usual time for faithful Li Hua to pay them a visit to deliver her little bag of coppers. They tried to reassure one another that she would come, that she was just late, and any day now she would come walking through the mission gate.

But the days passed and then weeks, and everyone knew that they were expecting the impossible. Little Li Hua was gone. She would never again greet them with a smile after a long walk down the mountain.

Imagine their surprise a month later, when Li Hua showed up again at the mission gate. Everyone came running to greet her after her long absence. They were overjoyed—and Li Hua's eyes were shining too. Sure enough, she had brought along her little bag of coppers, but she brought something else as well—a wonderful tale of God's miraculous deliverance in the wake of the erupting volcano.

This was her story. When the mountain erupted, spewing smoke and ash from its summit, the villagers panicked. As the hot mudflows rolled down the slope, many ran screaming to find a place of safety. Li Hua's mind was in a whirl, but she couldn't make her feet move! She felt rooted to the spot, and it seemed as if she were in the worst of nightmares.

A fear gripped her like nothing she had ever experienced! She could see nothing on the mountainside that would stop the flowing *lahars* that were obliterating everything in their path—and she was in that path.

And Li Hua was sure she could not run fast enough to escape it. She could not climb a tree or a rooftop. She was not strong enough.

She watched as the river of mud inundated the village a half mile or so above her on the mountain. It smashed into the houses of bamboo and mud, knocking them over as if they were made of paper. Soon it would be her village's turn to be buried.

Others like Li Hua also were trapped in the village—mostly the old ones, the crippled, or the very sick. Like Li Hua, they could not run or climb to safety. They could not escape the impending disaster, and they knew now that they would die. Many stood watching the catastrophe, wringing their hands. When they saw Li Hua, they turned and rushed toward her for help, terror etched on their faces. Li Hua realized that they would die without the hope of a Savior.

These were the very ones who had made fun of her for praying to God and singing her songs on the Sabbath. They had taunted her for refusing to worship at the spirit shrines. But things were different now; in Li Hua and her God, they saw their only hope.

"Help us, Li Hua!" they cried. "Pray to your God, or we will all surely die!" They might have apologized to her and told her how sorry they were for the misery and loneliness they had heaped upon her, but, of course, there wasn't time for any of that now. The one person in the village who could have helped them get to know their heavenly Father had been the focus of their unkindness and bigotry.

But as Li Hua watched the streams of *lahar* cascading down the mountain, her own heart fainted with fear too. The wide bed of boiling mud was streaming straight toward them, with its churning mass toppling trees and swallowing up gigantic boulders in its path.

She fell to her knees in the village street. There were only seconds now before they must all die; she could not get herself to safety, nor could she help those who cried to her for help. They would all perish in the next few moments unless God should somehow perform a miracle for them. There was no other way.

And then she remembered the promises of God. "My God shall supply all my need," she repeated once again as she had done so many times before. "Let Your angels camp around us," she prayed, her eyes now squeezed tightly shut. "Be our Shield and Protector."

A great sense of calm suddenly came over Li Hua as she knelt there in the street. A heavenly peace surrounded her, and she opened her eyes. The river of mud was now no more than fifty yards above her village, rolling along like a tidal wave. But at the edge of the village, the miracle began.

"Unless I had seen it myself, I would have never believed it," Li Hua told the missionaries, her eyes shining with praise to God. "When that mass of flowing mud came to the upper edge of my village, it parted and went around us. It divided like the Red Sea for Moses and the Israelites. Most had fled the village when they saw the mountain explode, but I could not and neither could the old ones and the sick among us. And now God in His mercy had heard me and helped me." She wiped her eyes as she finished her story, and those standing around listening had to blink hard, too, at this amazing tale of salvation.

In this story, the mission workers saw the real reasons for their own faith. God is good, and He cares about our every need. Sometimes bad things do happen to good people, but God can and will deliver us from Satan's power. Most important, God will help us get through the hard times and strengthen our faith in Him as the Creator, Redeemer, and Sovereign of the universe.

The villagers had recognized that their miraculous escape from death could not be explained except by the power of the little woman's big God. He had done something big for them all and delivered them from certain death. It could not be denied or argued away, and now no one would ever laugh at her again.

"The village was shrouded in darkness for several weeks from the smoke of the volcano," Li Hua added, "but when the air finally cleared and the *lahars* had cooled, I set out on my journey to the city. I had to climb over fallen trees and mounds of rock on the mountain trail, but I was determined that nothing would keep me from doing my duty. And so, you see, I have come again to the mission to bring my tithe to God as He has asked."

What a testimony to the faithfulness of God's servants in even the most remote places on earth! And what a testimony to the power of our God, whose arm is not short to help His children in time of need!

For years, the tale was told in Java about the little old Chinese woman and her resolute faith in God. Li Hua had stepped out in faith to do her part as a Christian. She had worshiped God as she best knew how, had witnessed to her neighbors of God's goodness, and had given up the pagan spirit gods of her ancestors. She had paid a faithful tithe from the little God had given her, and He had rewarded her for it in a miraculous way that no one could deny. Surely God had been her Shield and Protector!

"He shall call upon Me, and I will answer him; I will be with him in trouble; I will deliver him and honor him" (Psalm 91:15, NKJV).

In Harm's Way

Part 1: Drafted

Siegfried stared at the letter in his hand. He had known it would come and had been expecting it for quite some time, but that didn't lessen the feeling of dread he felt deep in the pit of his stomach.

He read and reread the simple font typed across the heavy paper with the German military letterhead. "You are hereby given notice to report for duty to the German army at camp 42 near Frankfurt, no later than Tuesday, the 23rd of February, 1894."

Siegfried winced at the finality of the words marching across the page. His father needed him on the farm now more than ever after he had taken ill the previous November. But the German army would make no exceptions. Every able-bodied young man must serve his country.

A drizzle of sleet was falling as Siegfried stepped out of the door of the post office. "Why didn't You answer my prayer, Lord?" he mumbled, as the icy pellets stung his face. "I hoped you would help me avoid military service. You know the army is no place for a Christian."

Siegfried had mailed a letter to the army some months before, asking for an exemption from duty because he knew his beliefs would clash with military regulations. He was a Seventh-day Adventist, and he was sure that would pose problems for him.

He had determined that he would never carry a gun. Guns were for killing, and that was not what he stood for. Siegfried would do anything else the military asked, but carrying a gun was out of the question. He would not kill. He knew it wasn't in him to do such a thing. But in those days, the army made no distinction for men with religious convictions. The recruits did as they were told, or they faced punishment—often the firing squad, especially during times of war.

Siegfried would have been content to serve as a medic or a cook, but even those assignments would be tough to fill. And even if he were given a noncombatant role in the army, he would likely be forced to work on the Sabbath. Siegfried knew he could never do that either. Disobeying the biblical command to keep the Lord's Sabbath day holy was unthinkable because working on Sabbath dishonored the Creator of the universe.

He had wanted to go to school—perhaps a Bible seminary to prepare for the ministry. Some had urged him to go to Battle Creek College in America to train as a pastor. Going to America seemed like such a big decision, a place far away from home, his parents, and everything that was familiar. But none of that really mattered much now. School would have to wait; two years in the army was mandatory. He had no choice but to answer the summons.

The sleet had turned to snow now as Siegfried paused to stare up at the deepening twilight. "Why, Lord?" he mumbled again, but no answer came from the skies as he turned down the little country road toward home.

He broke the news to his parents that night around the fireplace. They counseled with him and prayed with him, but a cloud of gloom hung over them all. There was no question in their minds: serving in the army was going to be an ordeal for Siegfried.

"Please, Lord," Siegfried's father had prayed fervently, "help our son to be strong. Let him be Your witness, willing to stand for You through good times and bad, faithful to You no matter the pressure. We pray that many will come to know the hope of salvation because of Siegfried's witness. May You be his Shelter and Strength."

Siegfried reported for duty within two weeks, riding the 6:00 A.M. train to Frankfurt. It was a day's journey as train rides went in those days. The puffing steam locomotive pulling a string of railroad cars stopped at small towns along the way and picked up passengers at every station. Some of the passengers were soldiers, headed to Frankfurt as Siegfried was; but he felt no kinship to them. Most paid him no mind as they laughed and smoked in groups of threes or fours, and it made him feel all the more alone.

Around noon, another soldier got on the train and sat down beside Siegfried. He looked as uneasy as Siegfried felt, and the two of them soon struck up a conversation. Dirk was a likeable fellow, and Siegfried found they had a lot in common. They were both from small towns in central Germany, and like Siegfried, Dirk was an only child. By the end of the day, they had become good friends. Siegfried was sure they would be a big help to each other, if they could only be assigned to the same unit.

When the train finally chugged into the Frankfurt station, the young men climbed out expectantly. Grabbing their duffel bags, they asked for directions and then headed out of town toward the military camp. There was no transport waiting to take them the three miles to the military base, but they didn't mind after sitting all day on the train.

At the camp gate, they signed in and then lined up with a dozen other recruits. The sergeant in charge of the unit barked orders at the men just like Siegfried's father said he would. "Welcome to your new home!" The sergeant welcomed them sarcastically. Siegfried noticed the hardened look etched across his scarred face.

"Your time belongs to me now," the sergeant snapped. "Starting today I am your only family! I will be your mama and your papa. I will be your best friend. Wherever you go, I'll be there!"

He began circling the line of recruits. "You'll see me at oh-five-hundred hours for roll call. You'll see me on the training field during drills. I'll be on the firing range and on cross-country maneuvers and in the mess hall when you're eating food that's not fit for dogs. And when you cannot stand the sight of my face any longer, I'll still be there."

The sergeant stopped right in front of Siegfried. "By this time next week, I'll make you wish you'd never seen my face."

Siegfried knew his nightmare was beginning. This introduction was every bit as bad as his father had said it would be. The only bright spot was that Siegfried and Dirk ended up in the same barracks.

The sun was hours from rising when Siegfried heard the sergeant's bellow the following morning. And it was even earlier than the officer had warned them it would be. Four thirty comes early no matter what time of year it is, but February is never kind to a soldier that early in the morning.

They each did a hundred push-ups, hurried through an obstacle course, and then ran ten miles—and all of this before breakfast. By the time Siegfried got to breakfast, he was sure he could eat anything. And like the sergeant said, the food was nothing to write home about: runny oatmeal mush, cold sausage, and two hard biscuits. That was it.

Siegfried stared at the skimpy meal on his metal tray and wondered how he was going to survive on so little food. He would have even less than the other recruits because the sausage was off-limits for him. He had been raised to avoid that kind of meat, but without it he would have even less energy.

"What's wrong?" Dirk asked, glancing at Siegfried.

Siegfried nodded toward his plate. "You want my meat?" He felt like crying, but instead put a comical look on his face. Maybe this was God's way of giving him a chance to witness. He remembered his father's prayer when they first found out that Siegfried must report to the army, and decided that this was indeed his first test of faith.

"I can't eat it," Siegfried added. "God says we're not to eat such things, and I'd rather go hungry than break my word to Him."

"Your word? What word is that?" Dirk stared at Siegfried, a spoonful of mush halfway to his mouth.

"My promise to God that I'll never eat anything that keeps my body from being the temple of God."

Dirk just stared at Siegfried. "Tell me you're kidding. That's the strangest thing I've ever heard."

Part 2: "Just Shoot the Gun!"

Dirk took another spoonful of mush. "You're a great guy, Siegfried, but this sounds ridiculous. If you don't eat that sausage on your tray, you're going to starve."

"That or freeze to death." Siegfried almost laughed. "Without enough energy in the cold weather this time of year, I'll just have to keep moving if I want to keep warm."

"You're serious," Dirk replied.

"You better believe it," Siegfried pushed his tray away. "When it comes to things I've set straight with God, I'll never go back on my word."

Dirk continued staring at Siegfried and finally shook his head. "*Hmm, I get the feeling there's a lot more here than you're letting on.*"

"I suppose there is." Siegfried half-grinned.

"All right, then, out with it. I want to know about this whole crazy religion thing you're into."

"Are you sure?" Siegfried stood to his feet and picked up his tray.

"The whole thing."

"OK, perhaps we'll have the opportunity this evening."

Dirk started to laugh, but Siegfried was already walking toward the door.

When they returned to the barracks that evening, guys were sprawled all over the bunks. Some were reading or writing letters, while others were smoking and playing cards. Siegfried's and Dirk's bunks were in one corner, so that gave them a chance to talk quietly.

"What else is hiding inside that head of yours?" Dirk grinned.

"Well, *hmm*. You mean, what else do I believe that's strange?"

"Yeah, pretty much."

"OK. Well, for one thing, I believe that God is the Creator of all things. He made the earth and the sea and the sky. He made everything we see. He made you and me." Siegfried pulled his Bible out of the duffel bag he kept under his bed. "You can find the whole story here in Genesis, chapter one." He tapped his Bible.

"Yeah, yeah, I believe that too. Who doesn't?" Dirk replied impatiently.

"And I believe that all people are sinners; the wages of sin are death; and Jesus died on the cross to save us all."

Dirk's face grew serious. "Sinners, huh. I'm not such a bad guy. I've been to church."

"Doesn't matter how many times you've been to church," Siegfried replied.

"I've been to church a thousand times myself, but it's not about all the good things a person does. That's not what makes one good. Only Jesus can make a person good."

Dirk shrugged. "I don't know anything about that. Are you talking about praying and stuff?"

Siegfried nodded. "That, and giving your life to God. Asking Him to be the Boss of your life."

"I don't think that's for me," Dirk looked doubtful for the first time in their conversation.

"It's the only way it can be done, Dirk." Siegfried lay down on his bunk. "You can never do things halfway when it comes to God. It's either all or nothing."

"Oh, come on. I've seen lots of people being good in church, but outside of church, they do anything they want to."

Siegfried explained what he meant. "Either you're for God, or you're against Him. It's that simple. You're not fooling God, even if you think you're fooling people."

Dirk flopped down on his bunk too. "You sure do know a lot about the Bible. Where did you learn so much?"

"My parents raised me well, I guess. They wanted me to know the Bible, so they had me memorize lots and lots of Bible texts. And, of course, I go to church a lot," Siegfried added.

Suddenly, a whistle blew, and thirty seconds later the lights went out. There was no more talking between Siegfried and Dirk. The barracks were run by that heavy-handed sergeant, and he didn't allow any talking after lights out. But it wouldn't have mattered anyway. In a matter of seconds, Siegfried and Dirk were sound asleep.

The early morning bell was shrill and long, waking Siegfried with a start. *Where did the night go? Did I sleep?* Siegfried wondered. The only thing he remembered was laying his head on his pillow. "Did Dirk and I really have a conversation about spiritual things?" he asked himself sleepily.

But there was no time to wonder because the sergeant was already shouting orders. "On your feet, boys! We've got work to do, and miles to run!"

They ran and climbed and did push-ups all that morning, and in the afternoon they were sent to the shooting range. Siegfried didn't know what to do. If he went to the range, they would give him a gun, and he would have to practice shooting it. And if he practiced, they would expect him to train with it during field maneuvers. And if he learned how to use it, they'd expect him to carry it into battle.

Lord, I'm in a real fix here! Siegfried prayed. *This is going to get really bad really soon. Help me to know what to do! Help me to say the right things!*

Siegfried decided he would go to his captain and ask for reassignment to the medical unit or maybe even to the kitchen—anything to avoid carrying a gun.

But the captain wasn't in, and that left Siegfried with very few options. He would have to go to the firing range, or he would be hauled in by the military police for insubordination.

When he got to the firing range, the sergeant gave him a rifle and a few dozen rounds of ammunition. Siegfried tried to tell the sergeant that he didn't want to fire the gun, but the officer didn't have time for explanations.

"Just shoot the gun!" he shouted in Siegfried's face. "Point it at the target and shoot!"

Dirk was already firing away at the targets placed some fifty yards away, and he hardly noticed Siegfried standing there. Siegfried guessed that if Dirk had known what he was thinking right now, he would have written his army buddy off as crazy for sure. The business of not eating sausage was bad enough, but not carrying a gun?

Siegfried knew he was fighting an unpopular battle by being so different, but his decision was firm.

"What's the problem?" the sergeant growled when he came by to check on his recruits. "Something wrong with your gun?"

"Uh, no, sir," Siegfried blurted. "My gun's fine, but—I'd rather not shoot it."

"Not shoot it? Why not?"

"Because I think I'm much better cut out for the medical corps or maybe the mess tent."

"Oh, a pansy, are you?" The sergeant stepped up to Siegfried and stood nose to nose with him. "You've got one more chance to aim that gun and shoot, or I'm hauling you in for insubordination and dereliction of duty. We don't have time for these kinds of shenanigans around here. Now fire that rifle!"

"No, sir! I mean, I'm sorry, sir, but I cannot do that. Sir!" There! He had done the impossible! The words were out, and there was no way he could take them back now. Siegfried stood holding the rifle, the barrel firmly planted on the ground.

"Take this man to the colonel!" the sergeant roared to a military policeman standing nearby. "He's refusing to follow orders!"

Siegfried knew he was in real trouble now, but that was to be expected. A soldier didn't disobey orders in the army and get away with it. Everybody knew that. And yet Siegfried knew he had done the right thing. He was willing to serve his country, but he didn't want to have to kill anyone while doing it. *Is that such a crime? I have been raised to live peacefully with everyone, and now I can't give that up.*

Part 3: Locked in the "Hole"

At headquarters, when Siegfried was ushered into the colonel's office, he wasn't treated much better. "You say you won't carry a gun?" the officer roared. "What's wrong with you, boy? I'll teach you to disobey orders." He glanced at the military policeman and jerked his head toward the door. "Lock him up in the hole!"

Siegfried had no idea what the "hole" was, but he guessed it must be pretty bad. And he was right. The hole turned out to be an underground four-by-six-foot cell in the military stockade, with no windows and no light. The ceiling was too low for him to stand, and it was not comfortable to lie down for long because the floor was cold and damp. Siegfried could kneel to pray, though, and this he found to be a great comfort. He prayed often and fervently, pleading with God for strength to be faithful.

Gradually, his eyes grew accustomed to the darkness. The prison guard gave him bread and water, but that was all. Siegfried had to wonder if Isaiah had been thinking of him when he wrote the famous promise that your bread and water shall be sure.

When finally released three days later and sent back to his sergeant, Siegfried had to squint to shut out the blinding light of the sun. It was Friday now, and he realized that he would soon have another problem to deal with. The Sabbath would begin at sunset, and he knew he must refuse to work on the Sabbath because the Bible prohibited work on the seventh day.

The sergeant won't understand any of that, of course, any more than he understood why I won't carry a gun, Siegfried warned himself. He determined to remain faithful to his values and his conscience no matter what.

Siegfried hurried through his supper. He was famished after three days in solitary confinement, but again the meal was a disappointment. He ate the potatoes and beans on his tray; and though he didn't eat the bacon, he found himself staring at it longingly.

He was so hungry! How could he continue on like this with so much against him? The food was poor; he had been punished for refusing to shoot a gun; and now it was almost the Sabbath, which could bring another crisis.

The sun went down with no fanfare that first Friday night in camp, but for Siegfried it was no ordinary evening. The Sabbath had arrived, and he had no plan for what he would do when he was called for duty the next morning. He felt sick with worry. Why hadn't he talked to one of the officers or the captain when he first arrived at camp to let them know about his religious beliefs? If he had done that much, perhaps God would have been able to work out something for him. Now he would just have to deal with the events as they happened.

Siegfried tried to read his Bible; but the barracks were noisy and filled with smoke, and he was tired. He just wanted to go to sleep and forget about all his problems. Perhaps if he slept now, he would wake in the morning and find this was all a dream.

But again the night was short, or so it seemed, because Siegfried awoke well before dawn. It was the Sabbath, and more trouble was probably on the way.

He slid out of bed to his knees and prayed fervently for strength to face the day. There was nothing else he could do. The lights were still out, so he searched through his memory for verses of Scripture that would encourage him.

"Be strong and courageous. Do not be afraid; do not be discouraged, for the LORD *your God will be with you wherever you go" [Joshua 1:9, NIV].* *"I am the vine; you are the branches. If you remain in me and I in you, you will bear much fruit; apart from me you can do nothing." "If the world hates you, keep in mind that it hated me first. If you belonged to the world, it would love you as its own. As it is, you do not belong to the world, but I have chosen you out of the world. That is why the world hates you" [John 15:5, 18, 19, NIV]. "When they arrest you, do not worry about what to say or how to say it. At that time you will be given what to say, for it will not be you speaking, but the Spirit of your Father speaking through you" [Matthew 10:19, 20, NIV].*

One after the other, the verses filed through his mind, and he was glad now that his parents had required him to memorize so many verses of Scripture. The words were a comfort to him, calming him and giving him peace of mind. And yet, at the same time, they were like iron, harnessing his strength of will to face the day. *"If God is for us, who can be against us" [Romans 8:31, NIV],* Siegfried thought.

And suddenly, the morning's stillness was once again shattered by the piercing shrill of the sergeant's whistle and his growling voice. "Up and at 'em, boys! On your feet!" he shouted. "Last one out the door will go without breakfast!"

Siegfried was already dressed, so he was the first one out the door. Unfortunately, that was the only good thing that happened that day. Right after roll call, the men were ordered to shoulder their backpacks and go for a ten-mile run. And for Siegfried, that was when everything went to pieces.

"I can't go today, sir," Siegfried said calmly as the other men all headed to the barracks to get their packs.

"What do you mean, you 'can't go'?" the sergeant bellowed. "What ails you?"

"No, sir, it's not that, it's just—" Siegfried hesitated, afraid, but he knew this only made him look weak.

"Just what?" growled the officer. "Spit it out, soldier!"

"It's—it's the Sabbath day, sir. I can't take part in the regular schedule today. I must keep God's Sabbath day holy."

"God's Sabbath what? I haven't the foggiest notion of what you're talking about; but if you aren't back here in two minutes with your pack, I'll have you whipped—and that's a promise!" His eyes bulged as he commanded, "Now move!"

Siegfried took a deep breath. "I can't. God made the world in six days, sir, and then rested on the seventh day. He has commanded us all to rest on the Sabbath, sir, so that's what I must do. I cannot march today or go through the usual field maneuvers. I must honor God's holy Sabbath."

He felt stronger now for having given the little speech, and surprisingly, he felt calm. He knew he was going to pay a price for taking his stand on the Sabbath, but he didn't care anymore. It was like he had his second wind. Whatever came next would be all right because he had done the right thing.

The officer could take no more. He yanked his pistol from his belt and began hitting Siegfried with it. "You—crazy—soldier! I thought you were nuts refusing to shoot a gun, but this holy Sabbath thing is the limit! You're even stupider than I thought!"

Siegfried tried to shield himself from the sergeant's angry blows as the barrel of the pistol hit him first on the head and then on his back and shoulders. Again and again, the sergeant struck Siegfried, becoming increasingly angry by the second.

"You're just a private in the army," he bellowed. "Nothing more than that, soldier! You can't give orders around here, telling us what you will and won't do! You're just a number to me!" *Crack!* The butt of the pistol came down on Siegfried's head, nearly knocking him senseless. "I'll teach you to be insubordinate," the sergeant raged, as Siegfried fell to the ground.

The man had lost all control now. A steady stream of curses flowed from his mouth as he kicked Siegfried ferociously with his heavy army boots. The steel toes of the boots struck Siegfried's ribs again and again. The young soldier tried not to scream out in pain, but it was hard. He had never hurt so much in all his life! *Help me, Lord,* he prayed frantically.

Two military policemen rushed over to rescue Siegfried; but even as they dragged him away, the sergeant continued kicking him. Finally, the sergeant stopped to catch his breath and wipe the sweat from his forehead as he watched them go.

"Take him to the hole again," the sergeant shouted after the military policemen. "He's sure to get the firing squad for this one!"

Part 4: Back in the "Hole"

Siegfried was dazed from his beating, and he could feel the blood trickling down his forehead from where the pistol had hit him. He was sure he had at least one broken rib, but he had other more serious things to think about right now. He knew the man was angry, but a firing squad? And all because he wanted to honor God's holy Sabbath day.

Siegfried managed to stumble along with the military policemen as they led him to the military stockade. He was in trouble with the army now; but when it came to God's Sabbath, he had no other choice but to be faithful.

The firing squad was a common form of discipline in the army. Falling asleep while on guard duty at night could get a soldier the firing squad. So could petty thievery among the ranks, or refusing to follow orders from a superior officer. And that's exactly what he had done—refused to obey an officer. He might not want to desecrate the Sabbath by working on it, but there was no way to get around the fact that he had refused to follow orders. Now he was facing the consequences. Besides having taken a severe beating, he was facing the possibility of execution.

Siegfried's head was swimming! *Will I be given a chance to defend myself and explain my convictions about the Sabbath? Will I be given a trial, or will they just take me out and shoot me?* He had heard of such things happening, but he couldn't imagine it was any good for military morale. Then again, maybe the German army didn't care about morale. Maybe they cared only about obedience.

The army had a code, to be sure, and it was based on following orders. Everybody had to abide by it, or chaos would result. Siegfried understood that, but facing a firing squad for choosing to keep the Sabbath day holy?

As the military policemen threw him into the same underground cell, Siegfried tried to remember the words of warning and encouragement his father had given him before he left home. *"Serving in the army will be no picnic,"* he had said. *"Be strong, Siegfried! Stand for the right through good times and bad, though the heavens should fall. God will be your Shelter and Strength."*

Would the German officers want to hear those kinds of convictions in a military court? Not in a hundred years, Siegfried figured. His track record wasn't getting better when it came to getting along with his officers. Already his sergeant hated him.

Siegfried's head was throbbing from the pistol blows, and the pain in his side was excruciating. He gingerly sat down in the corner of his pitch-black cell, hoping the pain would subside.

"Back again, are ya?" a muffled voice asked from somewhere across the darkened prison corridor.

"Yup," Siegfried finally replied.

"What are ya in for this time?"

Siegfried sighed. "It's my Sabbath today, and I told them I wouldn't work."

The voice chuckled in the darkness. "I wish I could say I was that much of a saint."

Siegfried crawled near the keyhole so he could hear the voice better. "What are you in for?" He gingerly touched the oozing gash on his head.

"A fight. Me and another guy got to arguing, and he made me mad, so I threw a punch."

"Where's the other guy? Did they lock him up too?"

"I don't know. I knocked him out," the voice chuckled again.

Siegfried found himself chuckling too, in spite of his wounds, and for a moment he forgot his own problems. He tried to imagine the guy in the other cell, and he wondered if he was brawny and mean looking.

"Are you that guy they had in here just a few days ago who refused to shoot a gun?" the voice asked.

Siegfried smiled. "That's me."

"You're a tough one, but you'd better be careful. They've had other guys before who didn't want to work. It was that same Sabbath day thing you're talking about."

"Sabbath keepers here? How long did they have them locked up?" Siegfried swallowed hard. He wasn't sure he wanted to hear the answer.

"I don't know. Years, I guess. The longest one was eight years, I think. A lot of it was spent right here in the hole. Nearly ruined his health. Tough minded, though. You've got to admire him for hanging in there."

Siegfried thought about that. *Is this what is in store for me? Being shot by a firing squad is the worst, but will eight years in prison be much better?* He wasn't sure which he preferred and decided he'd rather leave that decision up to God.

"Help me to remember that suffering for You is an honor, Lord," Siegfried prayed. He recalled the story of the prophet Daniel and his loyalty to God in Babylon. He had refused to worship anyone but the God of heaven, and it had nearly cost him his life. But God had protected him in the lions' den! It was one of the most famous stories of all time, and all because Daniel had dared to stand up for God! *What a witness, what a testimony for God in the pagan courts of Babylon! Can I be faithful like Daniel was?* Siegfried wondered. *Can I stand for God as Daniel did?* He knew that he could with God providing the strength.

Siegfried leaned back against the cold stone wall of the prison cell. He had no idea how long it would be before they called on him, but he decided he needed to make a plan. He trembled from the cold as he sat there in the darkness, trying to put his thoughts together about what he would say should they give him a chance to speak in his own defense.

And then a verse from Matthew came to mind. *"When they deliver you up, do not worry about how or what you should speak. For it will be given to you in that hour what you should speak; for it is not you who speak, but the Spirit of your Father who speaks in you"* [Matthew 10:19, 20, NKJV].

Siegfried tried to relax. He realized that he didn't need to worry about what he would say. God would give him the right answers when the time came. Right now, he needed to rest.

And then he dozed. How long, he didn't know, but Siegfried suddenly awoke with a start, confused and disoriented, stiff from the position he had been sitting in. He heard muffled voices and the jingling of keys, and then he remembered that he was in the hole awaiting sentencing by the German military.

He tried to stand up in the darkness but bumped his head on the stone ceiling. He wanted to scream as the pain from the wound on his head and his broken rib shot through him again, but the guard never gave him time to feel sorry for himself.

"On your feet," he shouted as he dragged Siegfried into the dim light of the small corridor.

Siegfried's mind scrambled to remember the details of the past few hours.

What time was it? What day? How long had he been in the cell? He had no watch, so it was easy to lose track of time, especially in a place like the hole.

He had disobeyed the sergeant's orders because obeying would violate the Sabbath. He had refused to get his backpack and run his miles. He had been beaten by the sergeant and then sent to solitary confinement. Siegfried's mind suddenly focused. *The firing squad! Are the guards taking me to be executed? Is that where we are headed right now?*

The Holy Spirit brought to Siegfried's mind the unfair way his Savior had been treated—unjustly accused, unfairly tried, beaten, spit upon, and crucified as a criminal.

Siegfried began to calm down. This persecution because of his faith was all the devil's doing. It was all a result of the war between good and evil that had been raging in the universe since the day Satan was cast out of heaven. So why should Siegfried's circumstances be any different from those suffered by Jesus? When he thought about it this way, everything took on a new perspective, and he felt himself growing stronger. "Help me to be true to You, Lord, no matter what happens," he prayed.

Part 5: Charged With Insubordination

When the guards led Siegfried outside, he could see that it was early afternoon. He must have been in the cell for no more than a few hours. His stomach growled from hunger. He felt famished but tried to ignore it. This was no time to be thinking about food. He was about to face the firing squad!

But the guards didn't take Siegfried to the prison courtyard or to the firing range, where he imagined such executions took place. Instead, they took him to headquarters. As they neared the front doors of the imposing building, where the German flag flapped lazily in the cool afternoon breeze, Siegfried's heart beat faster. *What will they do with me here? Interrogate me? Beat me again? Sentence me to death, or to prison for years to come if I am lucky?*

The prison guards turned him over to the military police standing at the entrance to headquarters, who then took him to a large official-looking chamber. Six high-ranking officers sat behind a large wooden table at the front of the chamber, and at least a dozen other military officers sat in chairs facing the bench. A quick scan of the room told Siegfried that his sergeant was not among them.

The military police took Siegfried to the front of the room, where an officer told him to take a seat in the corner. This was no doubt the trial he had feared he would never get, but the looks on the officers' faces told him it wouldn't likely be a fair one. And yet Siegfried felt calm. God was answering his prayer for peace and the presence of mind to be strong.

"Young man, state your full name and service number," the commanding officer behind the large table ordered. The bars and medals on his uniform told Siegfried he must be a high-ranking colonel.

"Siegfried Herman Kaufman, 02099596," Siegfried said without hesitation.

"You have been brought here on charges of insubordination to an officer," the colonel said curtly. "What do you have to say for yourself?"

Siegfried took a deep breath. Every eye in the courtroom was on him now. "Sir, I regret the inconvenience of this case, and were it not for circumstances other than my religious beliefs, I would not have caused you this trouble."

"What do you mean by that, Kaufman?" the officer addressed him using his last name, as was customary in the army.

"I mean that my belief in God requires me to be faithful to the Bible and the truths I find there."

"And what truths are these?"

"The one in question today is my belief that the seventh day is the Sabbath. God created the world in six days and then rested on the seventh day. To celebrate His creation of the world, He sanctified the seventh day and made it holy. According to the Holy Scriptures, we call it the Sabbath today. God asks that we join in this celebration by not working on the Sabbath. He has asked this of me and all men, and I cannot disobey His command."

Absolute silence filled the courtroom. Finally, the colonel cleared his throat, "This belief of yours? Is it in the Bible?"

"It is, sir."

"Do you own a copy?"

"Yes, sir."

"And you have proof in the Bible of this Sabbath command?"

"I do."

"And you can tell us where these commands can be found in your Bible?" The officer eyed him suspiciously.

"I can. The Bible contains many verses that speak of the Sabbath."

The colonel motioned to an officer sitting near the door. "Do we have a copy of the Bible in camp, Lieutenant?"

"I'll see if we can get one, sir." The lieutenant saluted and quickly left the room.

The colonel stared at Siegfried silently for several long moments. "Kaufman," he continued, "while we are waiting for that Bible, I'd like you to recite some of those verses you say are in your Bible. Can you do that for us?"

"Yes, sir." Siegfried looked directly at the officer. "Permission to speak freely, sir?"

The officer nodded. "Permission granted." All eyes were on Siegfried again.

"Sir, from the very beginning of the Bible, God has made it clear that the Sabbath is a holy day intended to be a memorial of His creation. 'By the seventh day God had finished the work he had been doing; so on the seventh day he rested from all his work. Then God blessed the seventh day and made it holy, because on it he rested from all the work of creating that he had done.' That passage is found in Genesis, chapter two, verses two and three [NIV]. God made the day holy, a sacred day for worship and rest, so we would remember Him and His wonderful works of creation.

"Another verse can be found in Exodus, chapter twenty, verses eight to eleven. 'Remember the Sabbath day by keeping it holy. Six days you shall labor and do all your work, but the seventh day is a sabbath to the LORD your God. On it you shall not do any work, neither you, nor your son or daughter, nor your male or female servant, nor your animals, nor any foreigner residing in your towns. For in six days the LORD made the heavens and the earth, the sea, and all that is in them, but he rested on the seventh day. Therefore the LORD blessed the Sabbath day and made it holy' [NIV]. It's clear in these verses that God is asking us to remember what He had already commanded thousands of years before, when He created the world."

Siegfried paused, but the colonel motioned for him to go on. "In the book of Ezekiel, chapter twenty, verse twelve, God tells us His Sabbath is a sign between us and Him. He says, 'I gave them my Sabbaths as a sign between us, so they would know that I the LORD made them holy' [NIV].

"Now the New Testament records that Jesus Himself worshiped on the seventh day. Luke four, verse sixteen, says that often 'He went to Nazareth, where he had been brought up, and on the Sabbath day he went into the synagogue, as was his custom' [NIV]. And that's not all," Siegfried continued. "God has promised us in Isaiah sixty-six that when Jesus comes again and the earth is made new, we will all continue worshiping on the Sabbath as we have done here on earth."

A rustle of whispers raced around the room at this latest comment until the lieutenant arrived with a Bible, and then all eyes once again turned to the front.

The colonel took the Bible in hand. "So why all the fuss about this seventh-day business?" he asked Siegfried. "Why Saturday, and not Sunday? I thought Christians worshiped on Sunday. Aren't Jews the only ones who keep Saturday for Sunday?"

"In God's eyes, the Sabbath has never changed, and you can find that anywhere in the Bible. I have dozens of verses that say it is so." Siegfried looked the colonel right in the eye. "If you find even one verse of Scripture that tells me Sunday is the Sabbath, I'll keep that day holy."

Part 6: Acquitted of All Charges

The colonel stared at Siegfried admiringly. "This hearing today has gone quite a different route than I had planned. You have defended yourself well, Kaufman. Very well, in fact. The irony of it all is that we're no longer talking about why you're here before this military court. It wasn't supposed to be about your keeping Sunday or Saturday, or Saturday for Sunday, for that matter. It was about disobeying orders from your superiors."

Siegfried looked down respectfully, waiting for the officer to continue.

"You know there have been others in the German army who troubled our military officers with their strange beliefs," the colonel began. "Some were imprisoned, some even executed.

"One young man here at this base told us he would never give in and 'break God's holy Sabbath,' as he called it. Didn't matter what we did to him. He claimed his father had always kept it and had taught him to keep it too.

"So we asked the boy if his father had been in the German army, and he said Yes. And in asking around, some of my officers said they thought they remembered him. Intense blue eyes, square jaw, strong as an ox, both in body and spirit. Stubborn as the day was long. Once he got a thing in his head, you couldn't get it out of him for anything. Spent three years in the military stockade for it, but even that didn't change his mind.

"The army finally said that if this man believed the Sabbath and wouldn't change, then we couldn't expect his son to change either, and we gave him an honorable discharge."

The colonel paused and glanced around the courtroom. By now, many other officers on the base had heard of what was happening at the hearing and had crowded into the chamber to witness the event. With them came the army chaplain, a Lutheran who was well acquainted with what the Bible taught.

"Reverend Conrad," the colonel said, "we have a young man here who has been written up on charges of insubordination because he refused to go through his military maneuvers. Claims he can't work on Saturday because that's his holy day for Sunday. Do you know anything about this sort of thing?"

"If he's a Seventh-day Adventist, he knows what he's talking about," the chaplain replied.

The colonel turned to Siegfried again. "Is that what you are?" he asked point blank.

"Yes, sir."

"If we're talking about Saturday for Sunday, he does have a point," the chaplain continued. "The Bible is quite plain about that. As to the charges of insubordination, well, that's another issue altogether."

The colonel conferred with his other officers on the bench, and then finally turned to Siegfried again.

"Before you came in today, many of us on the bench had decided you would likely be sentenced to the firing squad. This is the army, Kaufman. We can't have young recruits like you dictating how we run the army. I'm sure you understand that.

"That you are true to your beliefs is clear, Kaufman, and we respect you for that. You have made your point, and we know you can defend it. We need more men of character like you in the army." The officer shuffled a stack of papers in front of him on the table. "On the other hand, after much discussion, we have decided the army is not the place for you. You're just not a good fit, so we are going to sign your release today."

The room was suddenly abuzz with a sense of good cheer and perhaps relief that a serious miscarriage of justice had been narrowly averted. Officers crowded forward to congratulate Siegfried, and many inquired as to the verses of Scripture he had quoted.

"In the barracks among my personal belongings I have some Bible tracts on the Sabbath and other biblical topics, if you care to see them," Siegfried said. "Send someone to get them right now, and I'll pass them around."

A messenger was sent and was soon back with the little stack of leaflets. Siegfried handed them out, making sure the colonel who had presided over the hearing got one. In the end, there weren't enough tracts to satisfy the curiosity and genuine interest that followed Siegfried's powerful testimony in court. As it was, he had to write out some of the Bible texts for those who didn't get any tracts, and he even took the names and addresses of some officers so that he could send them all copies by mail.

And so Siegfried was acquitted of all charges against him and was sent home rejoicing to rejoin his parents. His testimony had been clear and his convictions strong. Like Daniel, he had stood for the right, and his superior officers had seen a young man stand true to his God.

A Second Day of Pentecost

Part 1: Ioana's Surprise

The wheels of the steam locomotive made a rhythmic *click-clack, click-clack* on the railroad track as the locomotive snaked its way through the foothills of the Carpathian Mountains. Pastor Johann Ginter leaned back in his seat and watched a big amber moon rising over the horizon. The train cars swayed rhythmically as they passed trees and hills, making the moon seem to dart behind first one object and then another.

Johann thought of his sweet wife, Andreea, back home in St. Petersburg. *Is she missing me as much as I miss her right now? Is she disappointed that I didn't bring her with me to begin a program of evangelism in Bucharest?* He would send for her when he could arrange a place for them to stay in Bucharest, but that might take months. *Is she wondering whether being a missionary in another country is worth the sacrifice of being apart for so long?*

Johann knew what it was like to be a missionary because he had served in the army when he was younger. The army either made missionaries out of Christians, or it cured them of being Christians altogether.

"How will we get along in Bucharest?" Andreea had asked him more than once. "We don't know anyone, and even the food will be different."

But food and friends were the last things Johann was thinking about. It seemed that the craziest thing about this whole adventure was that neither of them knew the Romanian language. He was on his way to Bucharest to become a missionary evangelist. How was he going to evangelize if he couldn't speak the language? Oh he could say a few words from a little dictionary he carried with him in his pocket, but that wasn't the same as being able to speak the language fluently, or even just the ability to answer the simplest of questions.

The lights in the train car had dimmed now, making the landscape outside more visible in spite of the darkness. The moon was riding higher in the sky, bathing the countryside with a velvety sheen. Its shades of orange had turned to yellow, and now almost white.

How will we reach the Romanian people with the gospel? Pastor Johann wondered as he stared up at the night sky. Somewhere past the moon and stars was the heavenly Father. At the moment, He seemed far away beyond the Milky Way and the countless galaxies scattered across the heavens. And yet Johann knew He was only a prayer away. The Spirit of God was everywhere in the universe, and yet was right there beside him in the train car.

"Father in heaven, my wife and I stepped out in faith and answered this call to take the three angels' messages to Romania. Show us how to do it, Lord. Help us reach those who are searching for truth."

The seats of the train car were hard, but Johann was tired, and the rhythmic cadence of the train wheels was beginning to make him sleepy. This train had no sleeper cars, but no one else was sharing Johann's seat, so he lay down to get some rest.

The next thing he knew, the train was breaking and blowing its long moaning whistle. Johann sat up and rubbed the sleep from his eyes. Shafts of sunlight pierced the eastern horizon as the steam locomotive with its string of cars pulled into the station.

So this is Bucharest, Johann thought. Multiple rows of tracks dissected the train yard. Johann grabbed his suitcase, stepped from the train onto the platform, and left the train station through its giant arching doorways. Immediately, he found himself standing in the streets of the capital city already coming alive with the bustle of a new day.

Wagons and carriages were rattling down the streets. Food vendors were setting up their stands with bread and cabbages and root vegetables. Burly men were unloading wooden barrels and boxes from delivery wagons at loading docks, and street urchins were darting in and out among the early morning traffic.

Where to go? That was the first and biggest question of the day. Johann needed to do so many things. First, he needed to find a place to stay. Then he needed to find someone who would exchange his Russian rubles so he could buy some food and prepare a good meal. He hadn't eaten well on the two-day train trip from St. Petersburg and was famished. After that, he would begin looking for someone who could teach him Romanian. If he wanted to preach and teach the three angels' messages in this country, he was going to have to speak the language well. Then, of course, he hoped that he might find Sabbath keepers in the capital city, but he had no idea where to begin looking.

By sunset that day, Johann had managed to accomplish the first three goals but hadn't yet found a Romanian-language tutor. He fell into bed exhausted that first night, with only a threadbare blanket to cover him on an old mattress in a cheap one-room apartment. He shivered from the cool night air as he tried to go to sleep. But the temperature didn't matter much, because the bugs sharing the bed with him wouldn't let him sleep anyway. Finally, he took his blanket and slept on the hard wooden floor.

The next morning, Johann hit the streets again and finally found someone who could speak Russian. The man took him to an office on the third floor of an old brick building, and introduced him to Ioana, a woman who agreed to teach him Romanian six hours a day for a price he could afford.

Simple conversations seemed to be what he needed to learn first because this kind of vocabulary would help him carry on the day-to-day business of living in Bucharest. Johann learned how to give simple greetings and ask directions and barter in the market. Learning the peculiar names of new foods was a real challenge: *sarmale, tocanita, salată de boeuf, papanasi*. Johann found himself missing his wife's cooking more than ever. The Romanian foods sounded delicious, but no one could cook borscht and pierogis like Andreea.

In the days that followed, Johann felt driven more than ever to study the grammar and vocabulary of the foreign tongue. However, at the end of three weeks, he felt he knew no more than when he had first arrived in Bucharest. It was so important that he learn the language so he could begin a series of meetings and establish a small nucleus of interested believers. Then maybe, he could send for Andreea.

One morning he and Ioana were discussing religion and the big churches that stood on the street corners of Bucharest. Ioana asked him if he was attending a specific church. Johann had been staying in his room every Sabbath and reading his Bible. He had not yet explored much of Bucharest and had no idea where to look for other Sabbath keepers.

"I'm a missionary pastor; but if I can't speak Romanian, what good can I do?" he explained. "That's why I've decided not to preach until I can preach in the Romanian language. God will help me," he added humbly, "but it would be good if I could find other Sabbath keepers in Bucharest to help me."

"Which religion do you keep?" Ioana asked.

"I am a Seventh-day Adventist," Johann replied, sure that she would have no idea what he was talking about.

"A Seventh-day Adventist?" she said the words slowly. "These people worship when?" Johann marveled at her surprising questions.

"Saturdays." Johann sat up a little straighter. "Do you know of such people?"

"Well, I have a friend who meets Saturday to worship. I do not know what church, but I know she goes Saturdays."

"Can it be?" Johann stared at Ioana in surprise.

"Why don't you find out for yourself?" Ioana said. She walked to the window and drew the curtain aside. "See that brown stone building on the street corner? My friend meets in a room there with a small group every Saturday morning. I know, for I have seen her go and come many times."

Johann was speechless. It seemed as if God was directing him to a group of

Sabbath keepers already meeting in Bucharest. The odds of finding Sabbath keepers on his own among a quarter of a million people would have been slim.

Part 2: Why All the Chairs?

When church leaders at the General Conference of Seventh-day Adventists in America had asked Johann to go to Romania as a missionary evangelist, they had said nothing about there being any Sabbath keepers in the metropolis of Bucharest. Sabbath-keeping Jews could be found here and there across Europe, but, in 1904, no Seventh-day Adventists were known to exist in Romania. Johann was well aware that presenting the three angels' messages in this part of the world was still in its infant stage.

But now Ioana was telling Johann she was sure Sabbath keepers worshiped here in this community. He could hardly wait to find out!

Two days later, Johann found sixteen Sabbath keepers meeting on the second floor of the building across the street, just as Ioana said he would. They did not know about Seventh-day Adventists and did not call themselves by that name, but they were worshiping on Saturday, as the Bible taught.

They had many questions for Johann about the Bible that first Sabbath morning together, but could not speak enough Romanian yet to be of much help. In their eyes, he could see the genuine looks of appreciation that he had come, as they held up a Bible excitedly and pointed at him.

Johann went home at the end of the day thrilled that he had found other Sabbath keepers, but he was frustrated that he could not yet speak their language. He had the words of life that could feed their souls, but he knew so little Romanian with which to share that hope.

Early the next morning—Johann had not yet finished his breakfast of bread and boiled cabbage—there was a knock on the door. He was surprised to see Emilian and Cornel, two elders from the church group he had visited the day before. With them was a young girl fourteen or fifteen years of age.

"Helga, Helga." The two elders pointed at the girl, and it was obvious they had brought her along to translate for them.

"I come . . . help speak," she said in her broken Russian after several awkward moments of silence, and she really did try her best.

Satisfied that they would now be understood, the two elders began speaking rapidly, and Helga found herself overwhelmed in her efforts to keep up. Emilian and Cornel greeted Johann warmly and apologized for a visit at such an hour, and then came straight to the point.

"We glad you come," Helga translated slowly and deliberately. "God, He send you for us."

Johann nodded and smiled. *"Slava Boag!"* he responded in Russian. "Praise the Lord our God!"

"We meet at church . . . at last night." Helga stumbled over the words. "Until late. We want Bible—the Word our God. You teach this Word for us," she continued, and all the while the two elders were watching Johann intently. "We know small Bible . . . and you know much. You bring joy in . . . our hearts. After meeting, we pray and talk at home. Elder Cornel's home. Sleep . . . no sleep much for pray."

Johann listened very patiently, but was having a hard time understanding what they wanted of him. It was all so frustrating, but what could he do? Johann was the one who didn't know the Romanian language. Living in their country, it was his responsibility to bridge the communication gap.

All three of them were looking at Johann by now. "We church want you for teach us Word of God. We have two Bible and learn quickly."

"How you say in Russian?" they looked at each other to find the right words. "We have meetings. You teach everything."

Johann waited for them to continue explaining, but they stopped now and waited for his answer. He stared at them in confusion, and then suddenly it came to him what they were asking.

He pointed at himself. "You want me to meet with you to study the Bible?"

Helga gave him a big smile and did her best to translate his words back to the two elders. "Yes," the two elders nodded quickly. "Please. We very happy for you come. We tell friends and they can come too. No?"

"At your church? On Sabbath?" Johann was getting worried. How could he teach these people about the Bible? He knew almost no Romanian, and Helga obviously did not know enough Russian.

"Yes, church." They nodded excitedly. "But not Sabbath only. Other days. Is why we have big room. Big for us, not big for God. He bless with more people come worship."

Johann was impressed with their faith, but he was also quite worried. This was not just a simple Bible study they were expecting. It sounded like a regular, full-blown evangelistic series of meetings. "You want to hold many evangelistic meetings?" Johann stammered. "Many meetings at night!"

"Yes," they grew even more excited now, and their eyes sparkled with anticipation.

"You want to hold public meetings for me to preach from the Bible?" The elders nodded solemnly at Johann. "Oh, but that is not possible!" Johann protested emphatically. "Who will translate? I do not speak enough Romanian."

"Helga." The elders nodded in her direction. "She is translator for us."

"No, I cannot! We cannot!" He dared not be too critical of what they were suggesting, lest he hurt Helga's feelings, but her Russian vocabulary was just too limited. How could she understand the great themes of salvation, the prophecies of Daniel and Revelation, and the teachings of Paul?

But the elders were getting up to leave now. "Thank you, thank you," they kept repeating as they moved toward the door.

Johann followed them out into the hallway, but they had obviously finished what they came for. They were not waiting for more explanations. There was nothing left for Johann to say or do.

He watched them go. "How can I preach evangelistic meetings? I can't speak Romanian well enough! Lord, what do You have in store for me here?" Johann prayed.

The next day he told Ioana they needed to study more, so they increased their study time to eight hours a day. The schedule was grueling, but it seemed to be the only solution. "If I'm ever to speak Romanian, it will only be with blood, sweat, and tears—or rather with endless vocabulary drills, pronunciation practice, and grammar lessons." Johann chuckled to himself one evening as he trudged home in the gathering darkness.

When Sabbath approached, Johann knew he must again face the elders and other members. They would want to know his plans for the meetings they had in mind. He would tell them that he had lengthened his language lessons, and if he kept up his studies of the Romanian language and they all planned well, one day they could experiment with public meetings. Certainly, God would bless them.

But the timing in Johann's plans differed totally from what the Romanian Sabbath keepers had in mind. When he arrived at the meeting room, the church members welcomed him warmly. "We happy you come for meetings for teach everyone Bible," they announced.

Johann glanced around at the room. It was bigger than what was needed for only sixteen members, and he noticed that quite a large number of chairs had been added. More than the week before. A cloth banner hung at the front of the room, too, with Romanian writing in big letters, and there was a little lectern standing to one side. Very simple and appealing, but he began to get a funny feeling in the pit of his stomach. *What are all these preparations for?*

"We find another Bible," Emilian said happily. "We have three now, and we have surprise for you. We begin meetings tonight! God is good, no?"

Johann could not see the look of dismay on his own face in that instant, but he could imagine it. The members must have mistaken his look of shock for surprise, because they all broke out in radiant smiles.

Meetings beginning here, tonight! Johann sent up a quick prayer to God for help. Surely God was in on these preparations. He was beginning to realize that he was the only one lacking preparation. The people in this small group did not lack faith, and they certainly did not lack confidence in him. Johann only wished he had a tenth of their conviction that this was the right thing to do.

Part 3: "They Think You Speak Romanian"

Johann continued staring around him at the simple, but tasteful, preparations the Romanian people had made for the evangelistic meetings. He had held scores of evangelistic meetings in his life, but never one in which he didn't know the local language.

He also didn't know his audience. He had no idea how much these people already knew about the Scriptures and what exactly they lacked. How many of them had a mature faith, established on the teachings of the Bible? Did they have leaders among them who could preach when necessary or conduct Bible studies or comfort those who were ill?

And then the Holy Spirit helped Johann understand the situation. These people were not asking him to evangelize the city of Bucharest. They were asking him to evangelize them and their neighbors. It didn't matter whether they knew little or a lot about the Scriptures.

The small congregation worshiped that morning and then shared a simple midday meal. After lunch, Pastor Johann excused himself to go home and prepare for the meeting that evening. According to the elders, he was to have eight weeks of meetings, to be held every night of the week but Thursday. "We give you one night break for getting ready Sabbath," they explained.

When Johann arrived at his apartment, he opened his Bible and began to write some notes. For the first meeting, he would preach on the love of God. Nothing complicated. Now the biggest problem was the lack of a competent translator. Helga's limitations were obvious, and he knew that unless God presided at the meeting, his efforts would be a complete failure.

After his notes were prepared, Johann dropped to his knees by his bed. "Oh Lord, I am but one man!" he prayed. "I have come to Romania with the gospel. I know You brought me here for a purpose because You never make a mistake. What will happen tonight, Lord? I'm praying that You will speak through me and Helga. May my thoughts be Your thoughts, Lord. May our words be Your words."

He felt better after praying and thought he might eat a little something before returning to the meeting place, but then decided against it. "I have enough on my mind and stomach right now," Johann told himself.

When Johann arrived at the meeting place, the room was packed. The elders were there waiting for him; and to his surprise, six policemen were sitting in the front row, handguns on their hips, but Emilian quickly assured Johann that the police meant no harm.

"They come for keep peace," Helga translated Emilian's words into Russian, "and for make you not speak against government." Her eyes were big and her hands were trembling, but anxious as she seemed, Johann doubted she was half as nervous as he. Here he was, a foreigner among them, unable to speak the language, being watched by police to see if he might say something offensive against the state religion.

The assembled group sang two hymns, and then Emilian got up to welcome the people. He even had a kind word of appreciation for the police sitting there among them. Then he sat down again and nodded at Johann.

Johann stood to his feet, and Helga came to stand beside him. As he scanned the faces in the crowd, he realized there must be at least 150 people in the room. All the chairs were full, and people were standing along the walls. Some people were even seated on the floor in the aisles.

"Thank you for coming," Johann greeted the people as warmly as he knew how in the Romanian language. "I pray that you will be blessed as we study from God's Word tonight." Helga smiled faintly, relieved that she did not have to translate his first comments. But Johann soon ran out of nice things to say in Romanian, and then it was back to the translator.

"God is our heavenly Father," Johann began, "and He loves us with an everlasting love. The Bible tells us in Genesis that He made us in His own image, and that we are His children [Genesis 1:26; 1 John 3:2]." Helga translated Johann's words into Romanian, and Johann watched the faces of the audience for expressions of recognition but saw none.

Johann continued to read from his Bible the various texts he had on his outline, and Helga translated; but he could now see confusion on many faces in the crowd. It was painful to see—knowing the translation was weak, and the meaning obscured—but what could he do?

Text after text seemed to fall on deaf ears. Illustration after illustration failed to register with the audience. Finally, Johann sent another prayer heavenward. *Lord, what shall I do? The people are getting so little from this message with the poor translation. Please don't let this first opportunity slip away. Some may never come again if I fail to reach them with a message of Your love tonight.* And then, suddenly, he had an epiphany.

He stopped preaching. *Something is not right here,* he thought as he scanned the crowd for anyone who might be obstructing the work of the Holy Spirit. But he saw only the folded arms of the police and their expressionless faces. It was clear they were here only to do their jobs, but Johann knew they needed to hear the gospel story too. *If the devil is here tonight*—and Johan was sure he was—*then the holy angels need to come to my rescue to do battle with the forces of evil.*

And then Johann suddenly realized that he had not prayed with the people before beginning his message. What a disaster! Perhaps his neglect had allowed Satan to disrupt what God was trying to do here.

"Before we go any further, folks, let us pray to our heavenly Father that He will bless us here in our meeting." Johann bowed his head to begin the prayer. "Please, Lord, speak to us here tonight as You did so long ago in the early church. May our words be Your words. May every evil influence leave this room, and may we hear Your message. We pray this prayer in the name of Jesus Christ, amen!"

He paused and looked around the room again. Everyone was waiting to see what would happen next.

"God so loved the world that He gave His only Son, that whoever might believe in Him would have everlasting life." John held up his Bible. "This verse found in John, chapter three, holds the keys to eternal life. The Son of God lived the life of a poor man. He healed people of their diseases and brought them words of eternal life. He cared little for Himself. And when His enemies brought Him to trial and accused Him of terrible crimes, He was crucified. He died on a cruel cross to pay for our sins that we might have eternal life." Johann was speaking with real conviction now.

"And now today, these many years later, the words of Jesus are still true. God's love for us has never been greater. We can be thankful that He is preparing mansions for us in our heavenly home. 'Let not your heart be troubled,' Jesus says. 'I go to prepare a place for you. And if I go and prepare a place for you, I will come again and receive you to Myself; that where I am, there you may be also' [John 14:1–3, NKJV]."

Suddenly, to Johann's relief, he was now seeing smiles of satisfaction. In fact, many in the crowd had tears of joy, and all eyes were on him.

Johann turned to Helga. "What has happened?" he whispered to the young translator. "Why are all these people crying?"

She looked confused at first; but then after a short conversation with Emilian, she turned to Johann again and smiled. "People understand now as if is perfect. They think you speak Romanian. They understand much. God is doing miracle for them. Is all good and clear for them, and all wonderful to their ears."

The local police were surprised at what they heard and saw. Not once did they hear Johann speak against the state religion or its leaders; and in the end, they came forward to thank him. One of the police officers offered to teach Johann some additional Romanian, and another policeman was later baptized because of what he witnessed that night.

God worked a miracle for Pastor Johann, and all who witnessed it would never forget it. Many stayed on to kneel and pray to this Great God of heaven who hears prayers and works miracles for those who call upon His name. What began as a feeble human effort had turned into a powerful lesson about dependence and faith in God.

Military Missionaries

Part 1: Victims of a Purge

Times were hard in Russia during the years of World War I. Many men were away fighting in the war or working in shipyards or factories to build munitions for the Russian war machine. Food was scarce, and the Russian government had to ration supplies. With little money for food, young and old alike had to work hard to provide the basic necessities.

The Seventh-day Adventist Church in Russia also suffered during the war. The Word of God was precious in those difficult times. Few congregations had pastors, so much of the leadership fell to the lay people. But God was with His church, as He has been in every age. Small congregations of Sabbath keepers could be found scattered throughout the land, faithfully meeting in home churches and honoring God. The practice of worshiping on the seventh day put the Seventh-day Adventists drastically at odds with the Russian Orthodox communities; but the Seventh-day Adventists remained faithful to the gospel commission, actively winning souls for His kingdom.

With hardships on every hand, soon very little separated the rich from the poor in Russia. On any given Sabbath, poor peasants could be seen worshiping side by side with those who had once been well-to-do. It was an amazing illustration of how hard times and the Word of God could change a congregation.

And yet, even in their poverty, the people managed to save tithes and offerings. Many hid their tithe and offerings in walls, root cellars, and holes in trees. They hoped that one day a pastor would come to collect them. And God helped them conceal His money, for had they not been so careful, it's likely government officials or the state church would have confiscated it.

Seventh-day Adventists faced other kinds of hardships too. The Russian Orthodox Church claimed to be one of the oldest existing Christian organizations in the world and regarded other denominations, especially Seventh-day Adventists, as competitors. Admittedly, the Adventists were aggressive evangelists and took seriously Jesus' commission to baptize believers in the name of the Father, Son, and Holy Spirit.

During these years, Petrograd (now called St. Petersburg) seemed to be a special battleground for the forces of evil. The three angels' messages had come to this city early on; but wherever truth found in the Holy Scriptures is taught, Satan is especially active.

The believers in the two Seventh-day Adventist churches in Petrograd knew their Bibles well and were very effective in soul winning, or "sheep stealing," as the state church called it.

"Who do those Adventists think they are?" demanded the bishop when he learned that another dozen Orthodox members had "defected" to the Adventist faith. "From everything I've read, the Adventists are nothing but an upstart Christian sect barely fifty years old!"

"But they're very popular in town," one of his black-robed assistants replied. "It is said they gain converts by doing good deeds to those in need."

"Good deeds?" the bishop spat the words. "What do good deeds have to do with it? We help the poor during the Feast of Nativity and Easter. What more do people want?"

"I am told they preach a very hopeful message and are very spiritual," another priest added hesitantly.

"Spiritual?" the bishop was getting angrier by the minute. "I'm the spiritual leader of Petrograd. Do I look like an altar boy?"

The attending priests said nothing more, fearing the wrath of their superior.

In his ornate chair, the bishop sat thinking for several minutes longer. Finally, he rose to his feet, pulled his scarlet robes about him, and went to stare out the window. "They've got to go!" he said emphatically, plucking at his long, flowing beard. "They've been a thorn in my side long enough."

His eyes narrowed as he turned to the priests. "Do what you have to. Start rumors about them. Threaten them! Stir up a mob! Burn their churches to the ground in the dead of night, if that's what it takes." His voice rose in agitation. "I don't care how you do it—just get rid of the Adventists!"

And so it was that a secret pact was made to purge Petrograd of the Seventh-day Adventist "scourge." A campaign of whisperings started by Orthodox priests spread vicious lies about immorality, strange theology, and bizarre cult rituals supposedly practiced in the Seventh-day Adventist Church. Soon these stories were circulating in every parish in town. Newspaper articles were written to discredit this church of the Bible, and soon local merchants refused to do business with the Adventists.

The climax came early one evening as a drunken mob worked themselves into a frenzy and headed for the two Seventh-day Adventist churches in town.

The Adventists had been secretly warned of the mob's intentions and called a quick conference in one member's home to decide what to do. Some thought they should stand their ground and defend their property and their right to religious freedom. "We've got to!" they insisted. "We must be strong like Huss and Jerome in old Bohemia, who stood up for their right to preach the Word of God."

"And die like them?" others protested. "You should remember that both Huss and Jerome were burned at the stake."

"But this is our country too," the arguments continued. "We have just as much right to worship here as anyone else."

Back and forth flowed the heated debate, but the majority decided to flee the city. "Better to live another day to spread the good news of the three angels' messages than to die at the hands of a drunken mob," they said.

And so it was that by sunrise the next morning, not a single Seventh-day Adventist was left in Petrograd to represent the denomination. To any onlooker, it must have appeared that the state church had prevailed over the Seventh-day Adventists.

However, what appeared to be a terrible blow to the Seventh-day Adventist Church in Petrograd actually became the foundation for greater things. Though the state church seemed to have won the battle, God's plans for spreading the gospel in Petrograd were not defeated.

Part 2: Genya's Study Group

God has a master plan. He does not expect to win every skirmish in the great controversy. But He has already won the war at the Cross.

A few months passed and then something happened to turn the tide for Adventism in Petrograd. A new batch of military recruits was mustered into the training camp on the outskirts of the port city. Among these men was a Seventh-day Adventist named Genya Papanov, who was just twenty-three years old.

On his first Sabbath in camp, he asked for a pass and went into the city in search of the Seventh-day Adventist congregations, so he could worship God as was his custom. To his surprise, he was met with angry frowns when he inquired about Adventists. Finally, an elderly woman told him the sad tale of how the Adventists had been run out of town.

Genya didn't know what to do. He was far from home, serving in the Russian army for three years, and without a church. He would now be without the benefit of Sabbath worship with fellow believers. Where would he turn for comfort when he was discouraged? To whom would he go for Christian fellowship when he needed it?

As the days and weeks passed, Genya grew dejected, lonely for the friendship of fellow church members. Military life was hard enough as it was, but now without the camaraderie of fellow church members in the area, he was spiritually isolated.

Gradually, he began to realize that he was not behaving as a true Adventist should. Seventh-day Adventist Christians were to be lights in the world, cities set on a hill. They were to be missionaries for God wherever they might find themselves. Shouldn't he be a light at the military camp, sharing the good news of the gospel with all who would listen?

Genya gave the idea much thought and spent several days in prayer. Finally, he decided that he would indeed be a witness for Jesus at the military camp, even if he must do it alone.

The following Friday evening, he asked a few of his army buddies if they would be interested in studying the Bible with him. He had been reading his Bible since the day he arrived at the army camp and the men all knew it, but he wasn't sure how his offer of study would be received. To his surprise, however, three of them accepted his offer, and what a good time they had.

Genya made it simple for them, not sure what their religious backgrounds might be. Soon he discovered that they, too, were discouraged with army life; all of them came from religious backgrounds, though not from Adventism. Two of them, Pasha and Yuri, were Lutherans, and Vadim was Russian Orthodox.

It gladdened his heart to see his friends so interested in the things they discussed that evening: salvation, forgiveness of sins, and how to face the battle against temptation and win. They seemed to discuss something about everything.

"I enjoyed our study," Pasha said, after Genya had prayed for them all. "Let's do it again."

"I've never heard anything this interesting from the Bible before," Vadim admitted.

Genya nodded. "That's the way it's supposed to be. The Bible is the Word of God, His Book of advice on how to live in this world and how to follow His pathway to heaven."

"In the Orthodox church back home, I've never heard the priest read from the Bible," Vadim added. "They chant the liturgy, but I haven't heard these Bible verses before."

"Well, I'll try to keep from chanting here in the barracks." Genya grinned, and the four of them all laughed as they hopped up on their bunks, tired after a long day on the training field.

In the weeks that followed, Genya and his army friends studied a lot, sometimes four or five evenings a week. Friday evening was their favorite time to study, but Sabbath was a good day, too, and Genya encouraged them all to ask for Saturday as their day off so they could study much of that time as well. On Saturday, the barracks were empty and quiet most of the day because everyone was out on field assignments or away with a day pass.

After a while, the Bible study group had increased to nine, and with Genya, that made ten. They all joined in enthusiastically, taking turns praying to God and reading from Genya's Russian Bible. Not surprisingly, the things they were reading and discussing were beginning to change their perspective on God and

Christianity like nothing in their lives had ever done before. God's goodness seemed to be shining from every verse of the Bible.

When Genya introduced the topic of the Sabbath as found in the Ten Commandments and explained it as the Bible's original rest day, none of the men in the study group seemed very surprised.

"That makes sense," Yuri responded. "If God wrote it down in the Bible, why would He change it later? He hasn't changed any of the other commandments, has He?"

"Not a chance," Genya replied. "Fortunately, He's the same yesterday, today, and forever."

The men were beginning to see the beauty of the gospel as taught by Jesus and the truth about the three angels' messages of Revelation. Not everyone agreed on everything they discussed; sometimes they had questions that were difficult to answer, but Genya always helped them find texts that made the subject simple again. The beginning of evil, the fall of Adam and Eve, the promise of a Savior who would take away the sins of the world—all were topics that made sense. In their minds, the church was much like an army fighting the forces of evil with weapons, regulations, and a military code of conduct.

In their discussions, grace and mercy sometimes seemed to be at odds with works and the law, but the story of Jesus' death made all the difference—no matter which argument the men favored. Jesus' sacrifice on the cross seemed to satisfy everyone that God was fair, both in the forgiveness He offered for their sins and the good deeds He expected them to do by keeping the Ten Commandments. In the end, all of the pieces of their discussions seemed to fit together like a jigsaw puzzle.

"These are amazing discoveries," Vadim confessed one Friday night as they were studying. "My life has changed so much now that I'm accepting the Bible as God's Word. It makes everything I do in life more important—like I have a real purpose in living now." He glanced around his circle of army buddies and then at Genya. "Is there a church that teaches all these things we're studying, because if there is, I'd be the first one to join it."

"Actually, there is," Genya's eyes grew sad, and then he told them about how the Seventh-day Adventists had been run out of town nearly a year before.

"And the Orthodox Church was behind all this, I suppose?" Vadim questioned.

"It looks that way," Genya sighed, and then stopped midsentence as if Vadim had given him some sort of inspiration.

Part 3: "Can You Baptize Us?"

The next day was the Sabbath; and after their regular worship service, Genya took the group of men on a surprise trip into town to do what he called "a little witnessing."

"It's not right that we keep this good news to ourselves," he said. "I'm sure there are many in Petrograd who would like to hear the gospel story."

The men spread out across the town, visiting homes, working two by two as Genya had instructed. Because they knew the Orthodox Church's attitude toward Seventh-day Adventists, they were surprised at the reception they found. In many homes, they read the people Bible verses they had written out. They encouraged the people to be faithful to God and even prayed with them.

At the end of the day, the men met back at the barracks and told their stories, which seemed marvelous indeed. Each had an encouraging story to share. Their first adventure in witnessing for Jesus turned out to be a glorious adventure.

"I have an idea," Genya suggested. "Why don't we find a place in town where we can worship God each Sabbath? We probably wouldn't want to open old wounds by using the Seventh-day Adventist church buildings. But if we could find a place to worship in someone's house, maybe we could keep it more secret. There must be some in town who would love these Bible truths enough to meet with us every Sabbath."

"That's a great idea." Yuri clapped Genya on the back, and the others agreed. Everyone had found families in Petrograd who were receptive to the gospel story, and the idea of forming a church group in a town where Adventism had been banned seemed daring and exciting. Would it work? The success they'd had in just one day of witnessing told them it was worth a try.

The next Sabbath Genya and his army buddies went door to door again, revisiting the homes that had been the most receptive. This time they asked the people if they would like to meet every week to study the Bible. Twelve people responded to the invitation: a family of five, a young couple, three elderly *babushkas,* an old man, and Adrian, a seventeen-year-old high-school student who seemed to admire Genya and his army buddies. It was an interesting group, with folks of various ages and differing backgrounds coming together to worship.

The fledgling church company of twenty-two now met regularly in the home of one of the *babushkas.* Every Sabbath, beginning shortly after dawn, they would meet to study their Bibles; and then near noon, they would eat a midday meal together. Afternoons found them out doing missionary work in the town, tending the sick, delivering food or coal to those who were destitute, and generally helping those in need.

Within a few weeks, they were calling themselves Seventh-day Adventists, though they did so only behind closed doors for fear that the Russian Orthodox Church might start a new campaign to get them out of town.

Genya and his friends from the military camp were the glue that held the worshipers together. They did not have regular church officers at that time; but before long, the most basic needs of the church were being met by many of the young men in the group. Genya, of course, was the most knowledgeable and experienced among them, and he usually gave a short encouraging message each Sabbath. However, he understood that a church would grow only if the members were given opportunities to use their gifts and abilities in service for others. And that's exactly what was happening. Slowly, the young soldiers were beginning to show their talents.

Maxim was a real leader among his peers, quickly taking charge as a head deacon of sorts. Yuri was already becoming something of a Bible student and often led out in Bible studies. Pasha did well organizing community missionary work, and was soon leading out in their afternoon witnessing activities. All of these young men enlisted the help of the newest believers, and soon the little church company was working harmoniously together.

One Sabbath morning during study time, the topic of baptism came up while they were reading the story about Peter preaching on the Day of Pentecost. One old *babushka* seemed especially concerned. "It seems that baptism was an important part of the early Christian church," she said, as she pointed at a verse in Acts. "When the people heard Peter's message about Jesus' death and resurrection, they asked him what they should do," she said. "And what did Peter say? He said they should be baptized. 'Repent, and let every one of you be baptized in the name of Jesus Christ for the remission of sins; and you shall receive the gift of the Holy Spirit' [Acts 2:38, NKJV]."

The *babushka* glanced around at the little group of worshipers. "Is this what we must do to be saved? If it is, I want to be baptized."

The whole room was quiet as they all turned to Genya, and he finally nodded. "It's true, Jesus gave us His example when He was baptized by John the Baptist. And He asks that we also be baptized to represent washing away of our sins and beginning new lives in Jesus."

"Have you been baptized?" the little *babushka* asked, looking intently at Genya.

"Yes, I have. I was baptized when I was fifteen, some eight years ago, and it was the best decision of my life. I shall never forget the day. Some of you have been baptized as babies since that is the custom of many Christian churches today. But God wants you to make a decision for Him as an adult. That's what really counts."

"I agree." Maxim nodded. "So how do we do this? Does it have to be done by a priest?"

Genya nodded. "A pastor or anyone who is ordained to be a leader of a church can do it."

"Can you baptize us?" several in the group asked him all at once.

"I am not a pastor," Genya replied, "and I am not yet ordained as an elder in the church."

"Then we must find one who will do this," Yuri said quietly, "because we must all be baptized."

"God will provide for us when the time is right," Genya added. "When we have studied and know more about what Jesus would teach us, then we will be ready for baptism." These words of wisdom seemed to be enough for the group, and they finished the morning worship with the story of the jailer in Philippi and his decision to accept Jesus through baptism.

The afternoon was spent doing more missionary work, and then the young soldiers headed back to the army camp.

Unfortunately, that very next week, bad news came from the city. Adrian, the young high-school student in their church company, came running to the army camp with a message for Genya and the others. The local Orthodox bishop had discovered that Genya and his army buddies had fanned the flames of Adventism in Petrograd again, and he was furious.

Genya and the others didn't know quite what to do when they heard the news, so they did the only thing they could think of: they prayed. That night the ten young men knelt in a circle and petitioned the Almighty God for His support of their missionary efforts in Petrograd.

"Please, Father," Genya begged, "don't let Satan win this battle. We have started to spread the good news of the gospel in Petrograd, and we want to do it all for Your honor and glory. For the sake of the new believers and the sake of the gospel, please turn aside the evil designs of the Orthodox leaders in town."

Part 4: The Mayor Sides With the Adventists

Back at his headquarters, the Orthodox bishop was once again calling his priests together. How best could they eradicate the influence of the new group of Adventist believers in the city? "The stories in the papers worked well a couple of years ago," the bishop said, "but I don't think we should go that route this time around. We need something that will run them out of town immediately."

"How about another mob?" ventured a priest.

The bishop thought for a moment. "Maybe, but last time it did have its bad side, and that doesn't always go over well with the authorities. It was too messy. We're lucky there wasn't a backlash over it all."

"Well, then, why not stage a peaceful parade of protest and march down to the parliament building?" suggested another priest. "As we did last time, we can demand that the Adventists disband their group. We can say the Adventists are enemies of the state church and are not good for the city of Petrograd."

"That might work," the bishop said hesitantly. The Orthodox Church itself was having trouble at that time with the local government and with the Bolshevik revolutionary forces of Russia. The persecution of Seventh-day Adventists might seem to be a brash statement of religious intolerance. If they weren't careful, that could backfire on them; and then the Russian Orthodox Church would come under fire too. What guarantees did they have that the government would continue to grant religious freedom to them as Orthodox worshipers?

For centuries, the Orthodox Church had been a powerful religious force within the country, but the new Communist leaders did not respect religious organizations whether large or small, and cared less and less about any alliances the church might have in political circles. If the Orthodox Church leaders could have seen the future and the direction their religious zeal was taking them, they might have been even more cautious in their dealings with the Adventists.

But the parade was planned anyway. Despite the bishop's misgivings, a day was set for the demonstration. Every priest from every parish in Petrograd and the surrounding towns was brought in for the event, and what a sight they made! There were scores of them marching four abreast in the street as they began their journey from the synod headquarters. Several miles down the road they walked to the *duma,* where the parliament met. The bishop himself followed along behind in his carriage, pulled by four matching white horses.

The parade of clergymen fully expected crowds to line the streets cheering them on, but no one showed up. The priests sang patriotic songs to show their pride in being part of Russia, but their hearts weren't in it. By the time they reached the mayor's office, they knew they had misjudged public sentiment about the Adventists.

The town leaders were waiting for them on the steps of the *duma* as the bishop drew up in his fancy carriage. Surprisingly enough, none of the government leaders said a word in greeting.

The bishop stepped out onto the red carpet his attendants had rolled out for him and looked around. His attending cleric unrolled an elaborate document and began reading in a dull monotone. The proclamation was an edict drafted by the Orthodox synod announcing their plans to eliminate the Seventh-day Adventists from Petrograd once and for all. "We are counting on the support of the top city officials to complete this campaign," the cleric continued, but still no one on the steps of the *duma* said a word.

When the cleric finished reading the document, the city mayor stepped forward. "We regret that you have come all this way to impress us," he announced, "and we wish to make it clear where we stand. The Adventists are a good people and have established themselves as fine citizens of this city. Why just this last week, my mother told me of the things she has heard they are doing to help poor folks in this town: feeding the hungry, tending the sick, and helping the elderly among us. And you want to oust them from Petrograd?

"Let it be known this day, we are glad to have the Adventists in Petrograd. They are much more effective than you are in keeping the golden rule: *do unto others as you would have them do to you.* I think it's quite clear," he added. "The Adventists are good citizens and are an asset to our city."

By the time the mayor had finished his speech, newspaper reporters had gathered and were taking down every word. The bishop and his train of priests left in a huff, and that was the end of that attempt to once again oust the Adventists from Petrograd. By nightfall, every newspaper in town was carrying the story on its front page, "Orthodox Bishop Scolded for Religious Intolerance!"

And so it was that God once again protected His people. The Seventh-day Adventist Church remained in Petrograd and grew stronger in spite of the flames of persecution. In the years to come, as Communism prevailed and the Union of Soviet Socialist Republics became a world power, the Seventh-day Adventist church members continued to let their lights shine as champions of the gospel.

Create in Me a Clean Heart

Part 1: Flee on the Evening Train

The story is told of Naomi, a young woman from a Seventh-day Adventist home in Damascus, Syria, who was quite attractive—and proud of it. She was indifferent to God. Nothing her family could say or do persuaded her to change her ways and give her heart to Him.

"Naomi, please," her mother would beg, "do not dishonor God! Jesus gave up so much for you. Can't you give up these worldly things for Him? Papa and I did not raise you to party like this. What would Papa think if he could see you now?"

But Naomi would not listen. She was angry with God for letting her papa die in the conflict between Syria and Turkey during World War I. She had been just fifteen when the war started, and her papa had marched away to serve in the army. It was difficult now to run the family dry goods store without him. She and her cousins, Nehum and Baari, had to help when they weren't in school, and some days they made almost no sales.

"Why did he have to die?" she screamed, when they got word he had been killed. *Why didn't God bring Papa home safely to us?* "If God can do anything, why didn't He protect Papa?" she argued with her mother many a time when her mother tried to reason with her about spiritual things.

"We do not always know the ways of God," her mother would counter, "but God is good, and He knows what we need. 'All things work together for good to those who love God' [Romans 8:28, NKJV]," she would add. "If we are patient, we will one day see His wisdom in bringing us to the places in our lives where the trials are greatest."

And Naomi knew deep inside that her mother was right. She knew that God had preserved them many times during the war. She remembered how He had sent angels to protect them during the nights when soldiers were storming the streets of Damascus. Kind neighbors had saved them by hiding them and had given them food when there was not a crumb of food left in their house.

Thousands died at the hands of ruthless mercenaries brought in to fight Syria's battles, and scores of Adventists were martyred for their faith in the attempt to rid the country of Christians. This cruelty greatly troubled Naomi and led her to question whether God cared at all about His people.

And now Naomi had recently graduated from high school and was wondering what she would do with her life. The country was unstable. One thing she was sure of, though: she was not interested in religion or the teachings of the Seventh-day Adventist Church. Mostly she just wanted to have fun. She wanted to forget about all the pain and troubles during the war. She wanted to enjoy life and make up for all the hard times they had been through; as far as she was concerned, being religious wasn't the way to do any of that.

Most evenings she stayed out with her friends instead of spending time at home with her family. Her uncle and aunt lived next door, and they often joined Naomi's family for evening worship. But Naomi did not attend family worships anymore. Time with her worldly friends was more important. Although she didn't stay out past the curfew her mother had set, her mother still worried a lot about her.

Uncle Lamech tried to reason with her too. Because Naomi's papa was no longer alive, he tried taking a fatherly role to control her. But Naomi was as adamant as she was belligerent. "I don't want to come to family worship," she said flippantly, when her uncle scolded her for not attending. "It's boring. I'll study my Bible on my own."

She didn't, of course, and had never intended to. It was just a line to get her uncle to leave her alone. As Naomi saw it, going to church was for people who had nothing else to do. Religion was for preachers and old people. It was for sick people or for those who wanted something special from God. But she was young and vibrant and thought she needed nothing from God.

Her friends were her life now, which seemed quite natural, because they all had so much fun together. She was not truly a bad girl, and did not do any of the dangerous things her parents had warned her about. She never smoked or drank alcohol. She was not romantically interested in the boys of her crowd; she just liked going places with them. She loved going out for ice cream and riding bicycles in the many parks in town. She loved walking down the streets of Damascus, looking at all of the things displayed in the shop windows. But mostly she loved going with her friends to the carnival near the market, with its carousel and games that were played in the midway.

Unfortunately, her preoccupation with having fun made it hard for her to see herself as she really was. Though she didn't see herself for the sinner she had become, she was now far, far away from living the messages of the three angels that she had once loved.

She disliked Fridays and Sabbaths the most because her family insisted that she had to keep the Sabbath with them. She attended the youth meetings grudgingly, singing only halfheartedly. She had a beautiful singing voice and had sung solos many times for church. But now her heart was no longer in it.

Of course, she should have known that her preoccupation with her friends was the cause of her indifference. How could she focus on the things of God when her heart was so closely entwined with the world? How could she pray to Him when she kept herself busy with her teenage friends?

"I'll settle down when I get older," she told herself occasionally when she felt the prick of her conscience, but for now she would not change her ways.

And then hard times came again when Sharif Hussein led the Arabs in revolt to take over Damascus. Religious persecution arose against all Christians, but especially Seventh-day Adventists because they were so different. Many assumed that Naomi and her family were Jews, and that made it even harder for them under the new regime.

One day Naomi's uncle told her mother they had better prepare to leave because it wasn't safe for them to live in Damascus anymore. He told them to pack a few things and to leave on the evening train.

But they never had the chance.

It was not even dusk yet when Naomi first heard rapid gunfire and the shouts of soldiers coming down the street. She and her mother were sitting by the door waiting, with a suitcase between them, when the commotion started. Naomi's mother grabbed her by the hand and rushed out into a back alley to escape, but it was too late. Soldiers swarmed up the alley; and when they saw the two women, they surrounded them, brandishing their rifles. Naomi's uncle and his family had tried to escape, too, but it was no use. They were rounded up and herded together like animals. The last thing Naomi saw of her family was her mother and aunt being taken away in one direction, and her cousins and uncle in another.

A dozen questions crowded Naomi's mind. *Where are the soldiers taking them? What will they do to them? Will they shoot them?* Of course, she was terrified about what would happen to her—and she didn't have to wait long to find out. The soldiers pushed her ahead of them down the street, shouting and firing their guns in the air. Other Christians were being pulled from their homes too; many of them Adventists. Some of the prisoners were loaded onto horse-drawn wagons; others were made to walk.

By the time they reached the center of town, several other young women were being dragged along with Naomi. She knew some of the girls well, but they were too frightened to talk to each other. The soldiers took her and the other captives to the local prison, where they were separated. Naomi was taken down a long corridor and put in a cell by herself.

Part 2: "We Know All About You Advents"

There was nothing in her cell but a wooden bench to use for a cot, a musty old blanket, a chair, and a chamber pot. The only light came from a sooty torch burning in the corridor outside her cell.

It was a cool spring evening, and Naomi shivered as she sat on the cold wooden bench. Fortunately, she was wearing a light coat, which helped some, but she was still cold. *What will become of me?* she wondered as she hugged her knees. *Why have the soldiers locked me up?* She had never been interested in politics, and she wasn't from an important family. Her immediate family members were Seventh-day Adventist Christians, and she knew that military officers weren't sympathetic toward Christians, but was that the connection?

As she sat there in the darkness, anger began to well up inside her. *What right do these soldiers have to take me and the other Christians hostage like this?* she wondered. *We are Syrian citizens. The soldiers have no right to do such a thing. Will there be a trial of some sort?*

Suddenly, Naomi felt braver than she knew she ought to be and jumped to her feet. She wanted answers to her questions. "Excuse me, sir," she called through the bars of the cell door to the guard who was part way down the corridor. "I want to know why I've been arrested."

The guard slowly shuffled toward her cell, a cigarette dangling from his mouth as he stopped to leer at her through the bars. "What have I done?" she demanded again, though she felt her courage wavering. "They have no good reason for arresting me like this!"

The guard took the cigarette out of his mouth and flicked the ashes at her. "You can just shut your pretty little mouth, miss," he growled. "Right now you have no rights!

"Sharif Hussein and his men will see to that. You're one of those Christian Advent people, and the government doesn't like you folks much. Your Advent boys are always making trouble in the military, disobeying orders, refusing to carry guns, claiming they can't work on Saturdays." He frowned and spat on the floor. "We know all about you Advents, and we've got just the thing that'll teach you a lesson."

Naomi backed away from the cell door. *What does he mean by "a lesson"?* The guard's words frightened her, and suddenly she realized just how foolishly she was acting. Right now, these people had her within their power. They could do anything they wanted with her.

She was uncomfortable to know that the guard knew a lot about Seventh-day Adventists. That frightened her because she remembered all the times the members of her church had talked about persecution against Christians. Jesus Himself had said that if His followers wanted to be witnesses for Him, they should expect persecution. And Seventh-day Adventists witnessed a lot. They were to be lights in the community and tell the gospel story whenever God gave them an opportunity.

But why was she was being punished for being an Adventist when she didn't even want to be one? Naomi was frightened and angry and confused. One thing was for sure. No one knew where she was, least of all her mother and the rest of her family, and she could only guess what had happened to them.

How long she would have to wait, destitute, in this prison was anybody's guess. Would the soldiers interrogate her? Would they beat her and torture her? Or worse? There was no one she could call on for help if that happened. Naomi didn't want to think about the odds—even death by execution was a possibility. As she thought about the dangers that surrounded her, she realized that the worst day of her life had come, and she was totally unprepared for it.

The hour grew late, and Naomi was exhausted. She lay down on the hard wooden bench but couldn't sleep; this gave her time to think about her life and who she had become. Being in a life-and-death situation like this was not a comfortable position for someone who had been flaunting her rebellion in the face of God and the church. "Why was I so stubborn?" she asked herself over and over again. "I know what is right, and I know I have not been living like my mama and papa taught me. God is good. The Bible is the Word of God, and not living according to its teachings is unwise, especially when I know that I really do need God."

And now she was in a real dilemma. How could she call on God for help when she knew she had been rebellious and didn't deserve His protection? The more she thought about her behavior in the previous months, the more she was afraid that she was in trouble with God as well as with the government—big trouble.

She had not wanted God in her life. That had been clear. She had stopped reading and studying her Bible long ago, and had even stopped praying every night before she went to sleep. She had not wanted any part of the church or the things that went along with being part of the congregation. She had not wanted to join the other young people at the Friday evening meetings. She had not wanted to go on witnessing adventures with the church members, or take part in the evangelistic meetings held at the church. She had not wanted to help serve the church as a young deaconess or be a Sabbath School teacher for the children. To be completely honest, she had not wanted to attend church at all.

God was not a part of her life, and she had been the one to chase Him away. She remembered the story of King Saul, how he had disobeyed the commands of the Lord, until God had been pushed right out of his life. In the end, the king had died a horrible death on the battlefield and was lost forever from the kingdom of God.

Remembering that frightening story made her start shivering. Like King Saul, she felt alone, alienated, and lost.

A tear stole its way down her cheek, and she brushed it away angrily. It was hard to face such fears alone, but it was even harder for her to realize that she was powerless to do anything about it. She had wanted to think that she was an adult and could make decisions for herself about God and the church, but it was now clear that things were not as they had seemed. All these months she had been fighting her mother, her conscience, and her God; now she could see that it had not gotten her where she wanted to be.

Suddenly, her mind went back to the days before the war, when her papa was still at home. She remembered the family worships and listening to him read stories. When he had asked her questions about the stories, she had always known the answers. When they sang songs of praise to God, she had known every word. When her papa prayed, she had felt the angels and the Holy Spirit in their little home.

The memories of those days with her papa were wonderful indeed, giving her soul a strange feeling of safety even now here in this prison cell. It was almost as if her papa had been a type of what the Father in heaven wanted to be for her.

Another tear trickled down her face, and the lump in her throat grew bigger until she could hardly swallow. A wall of tears was building behind her eyes. She blinked them back bravely, but it was no use. Suddenly, the floodgates of her emotions broke, and she began to sob. The tears came in blinding torrents, drenching her face and hands as she wept. It was a heart-wrenching scene, and there was no one to witness it, except, of course, her Father in heaven.

Naomi cried and cried until there were no more tears to cry. "What will become of me, Lord?" she found herself praying in desperation as she clutched her coat tightly. "No one knows where I am! I feel so alone. Is this to be the end of me, Lord? Is there no one now to save me?"

When Naomi thought of what the morning might bring, she sobbed, "Please, Lord, must my life end like this?" But from the darkness, there was no reply.

Part 3: "The Guards'll Be Coming for You Soon"

What have I done?" Naomi stared up at the ceiling. "All these weeks and months, I have brought shame upon my family and my home. I have been stubborn, willful, and cared for no one but myself. I have wasted my days, denying the blessings of salvation and the promise of a home in heaven. What a foolish girl I've been! How could I have been so blind and stupid?"

If she could have rolled back the hours of time, now she would gladly have thrown herself at her mother's feet to beg her forgiveness. She would gladly have listened to one more word of counsel from Uncle Lamech, or gone to the Friday evening meeting to spend time with her friends at the church.

"Lord Jesus," she prayed, her heart now broken and contrite, "please hear my cry! Please forgive me for my silly pride and my wandering heart. I didn't know what I was doing, Lord; but I realize now what I have bargained away."

The night had deepened now as she paused in her prayer. The only sounds she could hear were water dripping somewhere and the scratch of a match as the guard in the prison corridor lit another cigarette. The stillness of the moment pressed in around her, unnerving her. She could feel it like a shroud, blocking any ray of hope she might get from her cries to God; but strangely enough, something within her resisted the urge to panic. She knew that Satan was her real enemy now. She had listened to his tempting voice for too long, letting him convince her that a good time with her worldly friends was worth more than the values she had been raised with. Would she listen to his voice again?

She would not. She braced herself in the darkness with the same willful stubbornness that had gotten her into this predicament in the first place. But this time the stubbornness was for God as she got down on her knees beside the bench.

"Dear Jesus, I want to give my heart to You again," she prayed with a humbleness she had not felt in a long time. "I know I don't deserve Your mercy. I am a sinner, but like King David, I am begging You, Lord, 'according to your unfailing love; according to your great compassion blot out my transgressions' [Psalm 51:1, NIV]."

The verses she had memorized in church came back to her now like a wave of homesickness. " 'Wash away all my iniquity and cleanse me from my sin. For I know my transgressions, and my sin is always before me,' " she continued and was surprised that she remembered the verses so well. " 'Against you, you only, have I sinned and done what is evil in your sight; so you are right in your verdict and justified when you judge' [verses 2–4, NIV]."

Her tears began to flow again as she remembered with fondness both the verses and the feeling they gave her when she repeated the touching lines.

> "Cleanse me with hyssop, and I will be clean;
>   wash me, and I will be whiter than snow.
> Let me hear joy and gladness;
>   let the bones you have crushed rejoice.
> Hide your face from my sins
>   and blot out all my iniquity.
> Create in me a pure heart, O God,
>   and renew a steadfast spirit within me.
> Do not cast me from your presence
>   or take your Holy Spirit from me.
> Restore to me the joy of your salvation
>   and grant me a willing spirit, to sustain me [verses 7–12, NIV]."

Somewhere in the early hours before dawn, an amazing transformation came over Naomi. How long she stayed on her knees, she didn't know; but it didn't seem to matter, so intent was she on reconnecting with her Father in heaven. At last, she was feeling the peace she so badly needed. *God has mysterious ways of reaching His people,* she thought. *In my deepest hour of pain, He has reached out and touched me, even here in this prison cell.*

She had no idea what the sunrise would bring, but come what may, she would face it. She knew now she was not alone. The angels of heaven were with her. These hours with God had done something for her she had never experienced before. Naomi had turned her life over to God, and she knew she could put her trust in Him to care for her no matter the outcome.

The early light of dawn inched its way down the prison corridor, rousing the sleeping guard where he sat in his chair. Morning had come, and with it the uncertainty of the new day.

Naomi stood up and stretched her muscles. She was hungry, but she had more important worries to occupy her mind.

The guard stood to his feet, too, and came to stand in front of her cell. He lit up another cigarette and blew the smoke into her cell. Naomi choked on the smoke and tried to wave it away, but the guard just laughed.

"Well now, miss," he said with a toothy grin, "they'll be coming for you soon."

A sudden pang of fear seized her as she realized again just how serious her situation was. She had made her peace with God, but that didn't mean everything was going to be wonderful. The guard's words from the night before kept coming back to her, and she wondered what he meant when he said they would teach her a lesson.

"What do they want with me?" she finally asked, more frightened than she let on.

"Want with you?" he scratched the stubbly gray of his whiskers. "Don't know for sure, but I heard 'em talking about selling you in the slave market."

"The slave market?" Naomi exclaimed. "But I'm not a slave—I'm a citizen of Damascus and Syria!"

The guard began to roar with laughter. "Not anymore, you aren't." He slapped his knee. "With the new government in place, you'll be getting a new home, I'd say. A pretty girl like you oughta bring a hefty price for sure." The guard continued laughing as he walked away.

Naomi sat down on the bench. So that was to be her fate—to be sold in the slave market! It had never occurred to her that this was how it would all end. She had thought of interrogations, beatings, and even execution; but slavery? In some ways, slavery could be worse than death. In some ways, it was like a living death. The very thought of being bought for money and then led away in chains was terrifying to her.

Soon she heard soldiers talking in the corridor again. Two of them opened her cell door to lead her away. *Where are the others who were brought to the prison with me yesterday? Where are they? Will they be sold in the market as slaves too?*

The two soldiers tied her hands behind her back and took her outside to the street. They pushed her along ahead of them, laughing and snickering every time she stumbled.

Help me, Lord. She tried to be brave, but there was little else she could think of to say. Right then she needed to prepare herself for the ordeal ahead.

She knew that the slave market was by the gates of the old city wall, but she had never liked going there. Once she had passed by it with her papa when she was young, and the sight of the slaves being auctioned off had unsettled her. How could a man own another man—or a young woman, in her case? The thought of such a thing nearly made her heart stop, especially now that she was the one on her way to be sold.

The sun was well up over the horizon by now, and the rose-pink of dawn had given way to bright yellows and a blue sky overhead. New little green leaves were on every tree, and pots of colorful flowers decorated the windows of the houses along the way. Inside the homes along the street, she could hear people preparing their morning meals. An old man was singing somewhere inside a courtyard wall, and feisty sparrows chirped noisily in the bright-green foliage of a fig tree.

It all seemed strangely surreal to Naomi. This time yesterday she had been a free girl, making plans for the day to do as she pleased. Now she was a captive, her hands tied, and on her way to a life of slavery.

"Please Lord, deliver me from my enemies," she whispered. "I know Your promises are sure. 'God is our refuge and strength' [Psalm 46:1, NIV]." Naomi continued quoting Bible verses, which helped to calm her fears.

Part 4: "You Must Buy Her"

As Naomi and the soldiers descended into the lower section of town, people came out to stare at her as they passed. Some teenage boys made rude remarks, but she kept her head down. What a nightmare to be on parade like this!

Naomi's heart began to race when they reached the old city gate. She glanced around, but saw no one who seemed ready to be auctioned. Maybe there was some mistake. Maybe the soldiers had changed their minds and were not taking her to the slave auction after all.

She could see all kinds of shops lining the city market, each one staffed by potters, jewelers, or coppersmiths. Colorful awnings were being raised to shelter the vendors, and fruits and vegetables were displayed everywhere. A raised platform sat at one end of the marketplace, and Naomi wondered if that might be where the auction would be held.

She didn't have long to wait. Her hope dwindled when she saw several men talking near the platform and then point toward the city gate, where a group of women were huddled. Naomi's heart sank as she saw the looks of despair on their faces. If these women were slaves waiting to be auctioned off, then they were indeed the most miserable of all human beings. And in a few minutes, she would probably be forced to join them. She was to be sold as a slave here in this market too! She was no better off than these women.

"Help me, Lord," she prayed again to calm herself. "Deliver me from my captors! If I am sold as a slave, help me to remember that I actually am a child of the King."

A crowd was now gathering near the auction block, and the women at the gate were being led forward one by one. The auctioneer was shouting to the crowd and taking bids and getting some fine prices for many of the women. Women with finer features usually brought more money, but sometimes an especially strong-looking woman would bring a good price too.

Finally, all the women had been sold—all, that is, except for her. One of the soldiers standing near her shouted something at her and pushed her forward. Naomi stumbled and almost fell because her hands were still tied, but she managed to catch her balance and then climbed the stairs to the platform.

The auctioneer began to call out to the crowd, describing Naomi as though he had known her all of her life. The story he told about how they had acquired her was preposterous, but it didn't really matter because several men were already trying to bid for her even as he talked. The bidding was rapid, and soon the bids for Naomi had climbed higher than for any other woman's selling price that morning. And still the bidding continued.

Who were these men? It seemed one old Arab was determined to buy her at any price. She wanted to panic as she saw how persistent he was in his bidding, but then remembered her experience with God the night before. If God could give her the peace of mind she needed while alone in her cell, then He could give it to her now in the slave market.

Finally, only two men continued bidding. One was the old Arab dressed in fine clothes; the other was a hard-looking man probably in his thirties. A few more rounds of bidding later, and the younger man finally dropped out.

Naomi climbed down off the platform, her legs trembling, and her heart beating like a drum. *Why does this old Arab want me?* she wondered. *Does he want to buy me for work?* It didn't seem likely. She could not be more valuable for work than many of the other women who had been sold that morning. *Does he want me as a wife?* Older men often took younger wives, but buying one in the market didn't seem likely.

The Arab paid the auctioneer for Naomi and then led her away to one end of the market where he had a donkey tied. She could feel herself trembling. The Arab looked kind enough, but why on earth would he want to pay so much for her?

"Don't be afraid," the Arab man assured her, "you are safe with me. My name is Azeem." He had quite a story to tell. "All night I could not rest, and I did not know why," he told Naomi, "but this morning when I awoke, I had the strangest impression. God was telling me, 'Go to the city market. A young woman is to be sold at the slave auction this morning, and you must buy her.' I did not know what God had in mind. I did not know who this young woman was or how I would identify her, but I decided to obey. If He was giving me such a message, surely He would help me do the right thing."

Naomi could hardly believe her ears. Azeem had a twinkle in his eyes, and she guessed there was no other explanation for the miracle of her deliverance.

"And sure enough," Azeem added, "when I arrived at the market, I noticed you looking bewildered and in great distress. I knew there was something terribly wrong about your being in this place. There was no doubt in my mind that you were the one God wanted me to rescue. So you see, child, you needn't be afraid." He patted Naomi on the shoulder and gave her such a look of compassion that it made her want to cry. "Come along to my house now," he quickly added. "My wife will take good care of you. You look famished."

Naomi sighed with relief. God had kept His promises. Surely He had been with her every hour since her capture, guarding her steps just as her papa had taught her when she was a child. Surely her loving God had brought her deliverance.

Naomi stayed with Azeem and his wife, and in the weeks and months that followed, she was a great source of happiness for him and his family. When the war was over, Azeem helped her find her family again, but it was not easy. Sharif Hussein and his soldiers had not been kind. Her family had been relocated because of religious prejudice, so Naomi had no idea where in the country they might have been resettled, if they were in Syria at all. She later learned that her mother and aunt had been taken away to work in a clothing factory to make army uniforms, and her uncle and cousins had been sent to fight in the war. Fortunately, none of them had lost their lives; and in the end, she was blessed to have them all come home again.

It was a glorious day indeed when Naomi sat again with her family in the little Seventh-day Adventist church of Damascus. The hard lessons of her ordeal were providential, she knew, and had made an indelible impression on her mind. From that day forward, she was the most faithful of servants to God, telling young people everywhere that "the fear of the LORD is the beginning of wisdom" and "to obey is better than sacrifice" (Psalm 110:10, KJV; 1 Samuel 15:22, KJV).

Rain Man

Part 1: Finding a Meeting Place

Won Tak paused at the brow of a hill overlooking the valley. The day was hot, and he had walked far on the dusty country road, braving the midday sun. Beads of sweat rolled down his face as he stopped to rest under an oak tree. He sat down on a large rock, set his backpack on the ground, and fanned himself with his cone-shaped hat. "What I wouldn't give for a drink of water right now," he told himself. "It wouldn't have to be cold, just wet."

Nothing moved in the stifling afternoon. A lone yellow finch sat on a branch of the tree, its voice silent as if it, too, wished to conserve energy. Even the little lizards sat motionless as stone, eyeing Won Tak suspiciously.

A hot, dry wind rattled the brittle twigs of the old oak tree, giving it the illusion of a skeleton. Rain had not come to this region of the country in nearly two years, and the land was now parched and bleak. No crops would grow; there was no grass in the pastures; and even the trees were almost leafless.

Below him Won Tak could see the road he was traveling on and a small bridge that crossed the winding river in the valley. Just beyond the river was the town of Lu Geh Chuang, China, its red clay rooftops shimmering in the sun.

Won Tak wiped his brow with the back of his hand and bowed his head to pray over Lu Geh Chuang. Few Christians, and even fewer Seventh-day Adventist Christians, had entered this territory now ripe for the gospel story. The Shandong Province had long been a center of Taoism, Chinese Buddhism, and Confucianism, but the early 1900s promised to bring better days for Christian missions. A gold mine of souls now awaited the church—if the right workers could be found.

Pastor Won Tak was a Chinese evangelist and had long been working in China; but this was a new district for him, and he was excited about the possibilities. "Oh, Lord God of our fathers," he prayed, "if these people could just hear the good news of the three angels' messages, they would be the most hopeful people in all of China." Won Tak believed these words fervently, and his heart went out to the people of China who knew nothing of Jesus.

"Help me to find those who are ready to hear the words of life," he begged his heavenly Father. "Help me to present Jesus as the only name under heaven whereby we can be saved. Give me the right words to say, and I'll try to help Your angels in whatever I am assigned."

As Won Tak entered the narrow streets of Lu Geh Chuang, he noticed the marks of hardship and poverty everywhere. Because of the severe drought, times were difficult; food was scarce; and the little that was available was expensive. Shops were stocked with only the barest of necessities, but no one came to buy the things. The neat little piles of vegetables in the marketplace looked old and shriveled, and Won Tak was sure they had been there for days. But it was the pinched faces of the children that broke his heart.

Children should not have to suffer such pain, Won Tak thought. He knew Satan delighted in bringing misery to any land, especially to those regions where the light of the gospel had not yet penetrated. And without the promises of God, he knew these suffering people had little reason for optimism.

The water level in the town wells was dropping every day too. The elders of the region had never seen anything like it, and many feared that unless rains came to break the drought, a mass migration would be necessary.

But how could they leave their farms on which their ancestors had toiled for centuries? How could they leave their homes where their families had been reared for countless generations? The thought of such a drastic relocation made everyone sick with worry.

Won Tak had prayed that God would direct him to the right people in order to have a meeting in town, and he found just the person he was looking for in the marketplace. As he sat there waiting for God to direct him, he noticed an elderly man walking along with a small stack of books under his arm.

"Excuse me," he said as he approached the man, "could you tell me where I might find a place to speak publicly to the people of this town?"

The man appeared to be educated and knowledgeable, and Won Tak figured someone of such culture would surely know the best options in town.

"Why yes," the old man replied, "I think I can. I'm a school teacher, and you may use my classroom for such meetings." He bowed politely to Won Tak. "With times being so hard, we rarely get any good entertainment in town anymore. Are you the gentleman who will be speaking to us?"

"I am," Won Tak bowed in return, "and I thank you for the invitation."

"That's quite all right," the schoolmaster replied. "I'm on my way back to the school right now to continue my lessons with the children, but we are having a holiday tomorrow. If you will come to the school in the morning, you may use my classroom. I will spread the word that you have arrived and wish to make a public presentation."

"Thank you again." Won Tak was surprised at the man's friendliness. "I will do just that. Now could you be so kind as to tell me where I might find a hotel to stay in for the night?"

The old gentleman pointed Won Tak in the right direction, and before long, Won Tak had settled in to rest up and prepare his message for the next day. The "hotel room" was a veranda, with space only to roll out a sleeping mat, but Won Tak was used to such accommodations.

After he had eaten some bread and wonton soup the woman at the hotel provided him with, Won Tak opened his Chinese Bible and laid it on a little table by his sleeping mat. Then he knelt reverently before it and poured out his heart to his heavenly Father once more. Without God's help here in the strongholds of Satan, he knew this new witnessing opportunity would be wasted. With God's help, only Heaven knew how many souls would hear the words of life.

The next morning the schoolroom was crowded with townsfolk who wanted to hear what this speaker had to say. The window shutters were opened wide to let in any breeze that might be stirring. Those in attendance sat on the floor, as was the custom, and there wasn't an inch to spare. It seemed that everyone in the community had come, and the most important town elders were sitting at the front. They looked the picture of solemn dignity, wearing long-sleeved robes.

"We thank you for coming." One of the sage, old elders bowed politely. "We hope you have words of courage for us this morning. We surely could use them."

"I will do my best." Won Tak bowed in return and sent up one more quick prayer for God's guidance.

He opened his message with the story of Creation and God's part in making the earth and the sea and the sky. "The Lord God of heaven is the true God, for He is the Creator of all things," Won Tak said reverently. "Every tree, every flower speaks to His creative genius. Every bird song has been designed by Him to show us He is a God of peace and serenity. Every sunset paints us a picture of His character and beauty. He is God of all things, both large and small. The sun and the moon and the stars receive their orders from Him, and so do the little hummingbirds. Each answers to the power and goodness of the Creator God. That is why we must honor Him in worship, for He is Lord of heaven and earth."

The old elders listened intently to Pastor Won Tak's description of the Creator. It was clear these ideas were new concepts to them; and though they seemed to be enjoying his message, he could tell many were unconvinced.

"My God is a God of miracles," Won Tak continued. "Sprouting seeds are a testimony to the power of God. Birds migrating south, and then north again in the spring, are a miracle from God, for He tells them when to go. The birth of a newborn baby is a miracle, as any father will tell you." Won Tak continued, "We often take all these things for granted because they seem ordinary and happen every day of life.

"But my God does extraordinary things too," Won Tak added. "He can heal a sick child or make the blind to see, and He has even raised the dead."

"Ooh," the crowd murmured at these statements from Won Tak. Such feats of magic seemed incredible to them, and they were obviously impressed with the characteristics of a God who could do all these things.

Part 2: The Miraculous Rainstorm

What does this God look like?" one of the elders finally asked Won Tak. "He must be a most magnificent deity! Do you have a picture or image of Him?"

"I do not," Won Tak replied, and then paused, trying to choose his words carefully. "No one has a picture of my God. Jehovah is invisible to human beings. That's why we cannot see Him, but He can see us, and He can hear us from His place of habitation beyond the bounds of our world, in the Holy City called the New Jerusalem."

The gray-bearded elders looked surprised. They glanced around slowly at one another and then again at Pastor Won Tak. "But how can we worship a God that cannot be seen?" one of them ventured. "Does this not look a bit foolish? Will not people say we are worshiping the vain thoughts of our imaginations?"

"It might seem so," Won Tak said, "but the God of heaven is hidden from you and me because He is a Holy God. We are sinners in this world of evil; but when we worship Him, we become like Him in words of love and deeds of kindness."

"This is true." The old men were nodding, and Pastor Won Tak saw many in the room nodding their heads now too. "When we spend time with the great masters of Buddha, we truly become like them in philosophy and in our very attitudes toward life," some of them were saying.

And now it was Won Tak's turn to nod his head in agreement. He was very familiar with the teachings of Buddhism and the influence such a religion had on the local people.

One of the oldest elders cleared his throat as if to speak, and everyone turned to see what he had to say. "Honorable Won Tak," he said, "you have said your God hears us. My question to you is, Can we hear Him?"

"If we pray to Him, He will speak to us; if we listen, we will hear His voice. Sometimes it is in the quiet of our minds," Won Tak paused for emphasis. "And sometimes He speaks in words that can be heard."

"What does He say?" the old man asked.

"It depends on what you need," Won Tak assured the old man. "But one thing is sure, the God of heaven always speaks to those who pray to Him in their deepest need."

There was a long moment of silence in the schoolroom, and then the old man continued, "What can we ask of your God?"

"You can ask for any good thing in His name, and He will do it." Won Tak realized he might be setting himself up for trouble here, but he had no other choice. He knew these people led very simple lives. They and their ancestors had worshiped the gods of Buddhism for centuries and were not likely to be impressed with the ideas of some new God unless they could see evidence of His love, care, and miraculous power in their lives.

"Is it permissible to ask this true God for rain?" the old man asked earnestly.

Pastor Won Tak could see that the old man was serious, and he understood why. No rain had fallen in the province of Shandong for so long now that small children had forgotten what it was like.

"Yes," Won Tak said confidently, "praying for rain is common. In fact, there are stories in this Holy Book about such prayers." He held up his Bible. "I will tell you one of the stories right now."

At this, everyone in the schoolroom sat up a little straighter and leaned forward a little farther.

"Long ago in the ancient land of Israel, there once lived an evil king named Ahab." Won Tak began his story ceremoniously, and every eye was on him. "Now there was a drought in the land just as you are having in this province now; and King Ahab was very angry with the true God of heaven, because the drought had caused a severe famine among his people. For more than three years it had lasted, but God would not listen to Ahab's prayers or help him because the king worshiped idols of wood and stone.

"Now the God of heaven sent His prophet Elijah to the king to tell him to come to the top of a mountain for a contest to see who was the most powerful God in the land. So the king and all his priests came to the mountaintop and built an altar for sacrifice. There they prayed to their gods of wood and stone to burn up their sacrifice, accept their prayers, and end the drought.

"All day they prayed, but their gods did not answer them. They cut themselves with knives in their frenzy to be heard, but the gods of wood and stone could not help them because they had no eyes or ears.

"Late in the day the prophet Elijah built an altar, and he called on the God of heaven to burn up his sacrifice and send rain. And that is exactly what happened. The God of heaven sent fire from heaven to burn up Elijah's sacrifice, and after that He sent rain to water the land."

No one talked or whispered as Won Tak finished his story, and you could have heard a pin drop in the stillness of the schoolroom.

Finally, the elder spoke again. "Then we will follow this example," he said solemnly. "We will pray to the God of heaven for rain as this prophet did. Will you help us?" he asked Won Tak respectfully.

"I will help you," Won Tak promised. He had never before seen such faith among the leaders of a people who knew so little about the God of heaven. He marveled at their trust in a God they couldn't see, and his own faith was strengthened by their simple petition for rain.

The elders all gathered around Won Tak and followed the evangelist's example by bowing their heads as he sent up a fervent petition to God.

"Lord God of heaven and earth," Won Tak prayed. "You are the Creator of all things. We know that You hold the keys to sunshine and rain, and we are so grateful that You give us both. But now, oh Lord, we badly need rain. We humbly bow to You, asking You to send the rain to refresh our land and allow our gardens to grow. Hear our prayer, O Lord, amen."

It was a simple prayer inspired by the people's great need, and Won Tak could feel the Spirit of God moving in the little schoolroom. The Lord is all-wise and He would answer the prayer as He knew best, but Won Tak was sure He would send the rain. Had not Jesus Himself promised, "If you ask anything in My name, you shall receive it"?

Won Tak opened his eyes and glanced around him at the people. The elders were watching him expectantly as if waiting for his direction. The evangelist knew that he must seize this moment by faith. He closed his Bible and went to stand in the open doorway of the schoolroom. The elders followed him, and the rest of the people pressed forward as close as they could, as near as they dared. There was something about this Christian preacher they liked, and they didn't want to miss a word he said.

Then, too, a feeling of expectancy filled the air. It was a sensation of energy that made them tingle with anticipation at what was about to happen. After all, had not the preacher prayed for rain? If the stories he told them about the God of heaven were all true, then the rain would surely come. How could it not rain when the visitor had requested the Creator of heaven and earth to summon it?

Won Tak glanced up at the noonday sky. The sky was solid blue, and not a cloud was in sight. He shaded his eyes and glanced toward the horizon, first to the east and then to the west. And then far away to the southeast, he saw a small dark cloud sitting low on the horizon. "That is the answer to our prayer." Won Tak pointed at the cloud confidently, and he wondered at his sudden moment of inspiration.

"You think this cloud will bring us rain?" the elders asked him earnestly.

"I believe it will," Won Tak replied as he continued to stare at the horizon. "God has heard our prayer and is about to do something wonderful for the people of Lu Geh Chuang."

The people moved out into the street to watch the sky. The small dark cloud was moving closer. It became larger and darker, and a stiff wind sprang up.

Won Tak shouldered his traveling pack and turned to the crowd. "And now, folks, I had better be going if I want to escape the rain. I cannot stay, for I must make it to the next town before dark."

"Will you return again in the future?" the elders asked.

"I will, and next time we will celebrate the new life that rain has brought to your town." And with that he was gone, down the street, and out on to the little country road he had been traveling the day before. It was a fair stretch to the next town on his route, and he hadn't yet reached his destination when the rainstorm hit. The rain came down in sheets, drenching the countryside with the much-needed rain and bringing life and hope back to Lu Geh Chuang and Shandong Province.

Won Tak smiled to himself as he ducked out of the rain and stood under the sheltering gateway to a Buddhist monastery. "Surely, 'the eyes of the LORD are on the righteous, and His ears are open to their cry' [Psalm 34:15, NKJV]," he said, as he bowed his head in reverence to the power of God.

What a day this had been, and what a wonderful God he served! The harvest in Shandong Province was already ripe, though it had been planted only hours earlier. And now the showers of God's Spirit were falling fast. "Please Lord," Won Tak continued, "send more workers so the harvest can be gathered in."

Missionary Journey

Part 1: Paralyzed by the Witch Doctor

Thomas Sehare, the son of a Basuto chief in South Africa, was paralyzed, blind, and unable to speak. He had been in this condition for years, but no treatment was available, for this was the early 1900s. As far as the villagers were concerned, Thomas's fate was a curse from the spirit world.

Thomas had been a handsome young man, tall, energetic, and charismatic. Even as a young boy, he had shown leadership skills obvious to everyone in the tribal villages of Mafeking District.

And then one day, a white missionary came to Maribogo District, south of Mafeking, preaching the good news of the gospel. He brought Bibles with him and taught the young people how to read. He taught the villagers that they shouldn't have wild drinking parties or worship the spirits. Then he helped them build a small chapel out of dried mud bricks, so they could have a place to worship the God of heaven every Sunday.

Thomas's father, Chief Kabelo, visited Maribogo and saw the changes that had come over the people. He felt convicted that this was a new power he should have. The missionary offered to come to Mafeking and teach the chief and his people the words of life, but Kabelo would not make a decision on the spot. After he returned home, the chief asked Thomas what he thought of the new religion. Thomas shrugged and replied, "I do not have time for such things."

Old Kabelo sat by his hut for several days, deep in thought about the missionary in Maribogo. And then one morning, he announced that he did not want the missionary to come to Mafeking after all. He did not want to give up the old ways of his people.

What had changed his mind? No one knew; but it was rumored that Lenka, the tribal witch doctor, was at the heart of the decision. That, of course, was no surprise. Lenka had more influence over the chief than anyone else in the tribe.

No doubt the witch doctor realized that if the missionary came to the region of Mafeking, many people would become Christians. The Christians would no longer bring him gifts to contact the spirits. They would no longer come to him for advice on when to plant their crops or when to marry. The witch doctor didn't say much, but it was obvious he was afraid of the white man's God. If the truth were to be told, the God in the missionary's Bible was too strong for the witch doctor's tribal magic—and he knew it.

And so, although many would have liked to hear the stories the missionary was telling, the chief forbade it, and the missionary didn't come.

And then suddenly, tragedy struck the Basuto village. One day while Thomas and the other young men were out on a hunt, Thomas fell into a ravine and was injured. He received a bad wound on his head and became unconscious, so the young men carried him home on a litter they made out of branches.

When the villagers saw the hunting party returning with Thomas on a litter, the women started wailing. The chief called the witch doctor to Thomas's bedside, but there seemed little Lenka could do except apply a poultice of herbs to the wound.

The next morning Thomas still hadn't awakened, and the old chief felt desperate. What would become of his son? Would he remain unconscious indefinitely? Would he die? The old chief needed Thomas, for he was in line to take over as chief of the tribe in the near future. But there was nothing Kabelo could do to help Thomas.

All that morning, the villagers wept over Thomas as though he were already dead, but the chief just sat like a stone and stared at his son.

And then finally in the afternoon, Thomas's eyelids fluttered open, and he awoke. With shouts of joy people ran from the chief's hut to announce the good news. "Thomas is alive!" they exclaimed. But their happiness was short lived.

The young man couldn't move; when they talked to him, it soon became evident he couldn't speak. And then they noticed something strange about his eyes. They were darting about wildly, and it appeared he couldn't see. Many rushed to his bedside to witness the tragic sight for themselves, and soon they resumed wailing. This was the worst possible news, and to them it seemed worse than death itself. How was Thomas to be a chief if he couldn't get out of bed and walk? How could he carry on his tribal duties if he couldn't see or speak?

It was a pitiful sight to see the young man stretched out on his sleeping mat, his body motionless, his eyes now dull and sightless with no way to communicate. He could hear, but he could only make a few grunts and groans when he wanted to communicate. It was truly a sad fate for such a promising young man.

Chief Kabelo asked the witch doctor to do something, anything he could, to help Thomas recover. "I'll give you whatever you ask!" he promised.

But Lenka only shook his head. "He is troubled by the spirits," the old witch doctor said. "You are being punished because you visited the Christians at Maribogo."

The weeks and months passed. Everyone finally gave up hope that Thomas would ever be normal again—even the chief. In fact, no one paid him much attention anymore. Twice a day someone would come to feed him. He had to be bathed, too, but that was the only care Thomas received.

And then Chief Kabelo died. Finally, after many months of indecision, Lenka and the village elders assumed leadership.

Twelve years passed; and then one day, something most unusual happened that reversed the misfortunes of Thomas's life forever!

Three Christian African women from Maribogo came to encourage Thomas, pray for him, and give him a Bible. They spoke words of encouragement to Thomas and then opened their Bibles and began telling him the gospel story.

"Brother Thomas, Jesus loves you," one old sister told him. "That is why He came to the human race, so that you would know there is a Father in heaven who cares for you. This Jesus was a wonderful Man, born of a woman into this world, Mr. Thomas, and yet He was God's Son.

"Mr. devil man made life miserable for the Son of God with all the trials and temptations he could heap upon our Jesus, but that didn't make a difference to our Lord. He just went right on doing good for everyone, teaching the people about things they would need to do to get ready for His coming kingdom. He did miracles aplenty: multiplied the loaves and fishes, healed the blind and lame folks, walked on water, cast out demons, and even raised the dead." The old woman nodded emphatically to make her point.

"But wicked men did not like Him and wanted to do Him harm," one of the younger women added. "His own people finally turned against Him, Mr. Thomas. Can you believe it? His own people!" At this, Thomas gave a flinch of recognition to what the Christian women were telling him.

"Those folks mocked Him and spit on Him and whipped Him, but our Jesus never did say a word of reproach to them. That was because He meant to be their Redeemer and knew He must die for the sins of the world. They couldn't see it, but Jesus could. And when they nailed Him to a cross, He just said, 'Father, forgive these wicked men, for they know not what they are doing.' "

A tear stole down Thomas's cheek, for he had never heard of such a thing. That the God of heaven should do something this grand for the world was beyond comprehension, and it touched him deeply.

"Our Master Jesus felt all alone hanging on that cross," the young woman continued, "but He knew He must go through with it. 'God so loved the world that He gave His only begotten Son, that whoever believes in Him should not perish but have everlasting life' [John 3:16, NKJV]. That's our Jesus, Mr. Thomas. He died for you just as He died for everyone who calls on His name. 'Believe on the Lord Jesus Christ,' Mr. Thomas, 'and thou shalt be saved' [Acts 16:31, KJV]. 'Keep his commandments: for this is the whole duty of man' [Ecclesiastes 12:13, KJV]." The women repeated verse after verse. " 'There is no other name under heaven . . . by which we must be saved' [Acts 4:12, KJV]."

Part 2: Women's Prayers Answered

By now tears were running down Thomas's face, and one of the women wiped them away with her handkerchief. "Do you choose to accept Jesus as your God?" she asked kindly, laying a Bible in his hands.

Of course, Thomas could not speak; but he made a few grunts, and the women were sure now this was what he wanted more than anything.

"Would you like for us to pray for you right now?" she continued, and more tears came as Thomas groaned his response.

The women knelt beside his bed. "Lord Jesus, You have heard Mr. Thomas," she began. "You know his heart. For these many years now, he has been unable to walk or talk or see, and Satan has made him miserable, holding him in chains of darkest captivity. But Mr. Thomas wants to give You his life now so that he can have the peace of heaven in his heart. And please, Lord Jesus, heal Mr. Thomas's body as well as his soul. You can do this because you are the Great Physician who made him in Your image. Please heal Thomas now, in the name of the Father and the Son and the Holy Spirit! Amen."

The prayer ended, and the women stood to their feet. To their amazement, Thomas stood up with them.

"I'm healed!" Thomas shouted in excitement, as he jumped up and down. "Praise God, I'm healed! Thank you so much for praying to the Lord God Almighty. How can I ever thank you?" he said to the women, as he rushed out of the door of his hut and into the street, clutching the Bible tightly in his hands.

"I'm healed! I'm healed!" he kept shouting. "The Word of the Christians' Lord God Almighty has healed me of all my diseases." Then he raced down the street, leaping high in the air and praising God for this incredible miracle.

No one looked more delighted than the three women from Maribogo. But the shock and awe on the faces of the bystanders who came running to see the commotion was a marvelous thing to behold.

"How did this happen?" they all wanted to know, but all Thomas could say was, "The Christian women prayed, and Jesus has healed me!"

It was a day such as never before seen among the tribes of Mafeking or Maribogo, and everyone rejoiced at this amazing miracle.

That night Thomas sat up late reading the Bible the Christian women had given him. He was so happy to have his eyesight back that he couldn't sleep. Fortunately, he could read English because his father had sent him to the government school when he was just a boy. For several days, he read, chapter after chapter; and while he read, he discovered one Bible truth after another. He learned about Creation. He discovered the plan of salvation. He found the Ten Commandments and discovered that the seventh day is the Sabbath. The light of these revelations had brought a new day for him and were as exciting to him as his newly regained ability to see. After several days of study, he was a converted man, and he told his family and friends he wanted to give his life to the Christian God.

The family didn't know what to say; when the witch doctor heard the news, he came running. "You can't become a Christian in this village!" he shouted, but Thomas paid him no mind.

"I can and I will," he replied. "Jesus gave His life for me, and now He has healed me. I can't believe I ignored His Word when I learned of all the good it did for the people in Maribogo. Beginning today, I intend to show God my gratitude."

"And how will you do that?" his family asked.

"By honoring the Sabbath," he announced. "Tomorrow is the Lord's Day, and we must keep it."

"You must be joking," they all laughed. "We're not Christians. Why should we worship God at all, much less on the seventh day?"

"Because God created the world and asked us to rest on the seventh day as He did."

"Well, if you're going to honor God, worship Him on Sunday like all other Christians do," they said. "That's what the missionary taught the people over at Maribogo."

"Well, they're wrong," Thomas argued. "Sunday is not the Sabbath according to the Bible. In the book of Exodus, it says God rested on the seventh day and honored it and sanctified it."

"You're crazy!" they said, surprised at his determination. "Don't let the Bible change you so much."

Thomas was adamant. "I have to," he said solemnly. "I was physically blind before, and I don't want to be spiritually blind too." He pulled his Bible from the shoulder bag he was carrying. "The Bible says we are wretched, pitiful, poor, blind, and naked. I found that in the book of Revelation, and I believe it." He smiled with the peace of heaven on his face. "So you see, I cannot ignore God's Word and refuse to do what I know is right."

Many still laughed at him, and others went away shaking their heads; but Thomas was determined and kept his first Sabbath the next day anyway.

Soon he heard that a Sabbath-keeping missionary lived in a village some distance away to the southwest, and he longed to visit the man. "How blessed I would be to worship with a like believer," he told himself and decided he must go in search of the people who keep all of God's commandments.

And so Thomas set out on his quest. He didn't know exactly how far he had to go, but the folks he asked for directions kept pointing him west. As he traveled, all along the way he witnessed to the people in the villages, telling them about his newfound faith and of the importance of keeping God's Sabbath holy. Many laughed at him as his own people had done in Mafeking, and some even chased him away. He was surprised at this treatment. Wasn't he bringing the words of life to people who were living in darkness? Didn't they want to be released from their superstitious fear of the spirits, and from the tribal taboos that poisoned life's every decision? Didn't they want to be happy and receive the peace of God as he himself had been blessed to do?

It didn't seem so, but Thomas refused to become discouraged. When he was rejected in one village, he would set out again on his journey with a greater determination. He would find the Sabbath-keeping missionary. He would find like believers who kept all of the commandments of God. That was his one goal in life now, and he knew he would not be satisfied until he achieved it.

There were dangers along the way. There was the dreaded tsetse fly that could bite a man and make him go to sleep. "Sleeping sickness" was what the white man called it. There were bandits that roamed the roads by day, beating and robbing travelers, often leaving them for dead. And the worst dangers of all were the ones that prowled the countryside at night, looking for an easy meal.

But Thomas relied on God for courage and protection from every peril. Many a day he would walk along the road, repeating the Bible verses he had already put to memory. Nights found him beside a large campfire, reading his Bible by firelight and praying that God would keep him from harm. It was a time of anxiety and watchfulness, but the little he knew of God gave him the peace of mind he needed. He would press on; he would succeed in what he had set out to do. He would find the Sabbath keepers.

And God was good. When Thomas came to the region of Basutoland, he finally found the Kolo Mission Station. It was early afternoon when he reached the mission gate and asked where he might find the Sabbath-keeping missionary.

"Pastor Silsbee should be in there." A student working in the school vegetable garden pointed Thomas in the direction of a small chapel.

Part 3: Finding Sabbath Keepers at Last

Thomas dropped to his knees when he saw Brother Silsbee standing at the door of the chapel. His long journey had ended. He had found the man he was looking for. He was far from home, but, strangely enough, he felt as if this was where he belonged. And in a way it was, for this was where he would learn the truth of the three angels' messages.

"I have found the seventh-day keepers at last!" he shouted, raising his hands to the sky. "These are the people who worship God in Spirit and truth. I will never stop praising the name of Jesus for bringing me out of darkness into His marvelous light."

Then he told Brother Silsbee about his miraculous story of healing, of how he had discovered the Sabbath, and why he had come to Basutoland. The two talked all afternoon, stopping only long enough at suppertime to eat the squash and maize porridge the pastor's wife had made for them. Even while they ate, they exchanged ideas as they read verse after verse in the Bible. Thomas felt as if he were feasting at a banquet.

He told Pastor Silsbee what he knew about the Sabbath, and then asked about the rest of the commandments. "I read here in James, chapter two, verse ten, that if I keep all but one, I am guilty of breaking them all. How can this be?"

Pastor Silsbee smiled and laid a hand on Thomas's shoulder, "It is because the commandments represent God's character, and He is perfect. God cannot be perfect in only some parts of His law. He is perfectly holy, and so is His law. If we would truly obey Him in our hearts and souls, we must do so completely by obeying all of His commandments."

"Then who can be saved?" Thomas protested in surprise. "I want to serve God, and I want to love Him with all of my heart, but I know I will make mistakes. I am a sinner man."

"Ah, my friend, that is the beauty of the gospel," Pastor Silsbee assured him. "You see, we cannot keep the commandments of God on our own. You are right, it can't be done. But we can ask Jesus to help us, and He will give us the strength to keep them. 'I can do all things through Christ who strengthens me' [NKJV]." Pastor Silsbee read the famous verse from Philippians 4:13, and Thomas was humbled at such a thought.

"So then every day Jesus will make me strong to resist Satan's temptations?" Thomas asked. "And day by day, I will become more like the Father in heaven?"

"That's exactly right." Pastor Silsbee nodded. "And with that little bit of knowledge alone, you are very near the kingdom of God, Brother Thomas."

They talked about life after death, and Thomas truly was confused when Pastor Silsbee told him that people stay in the grave when they die.

"How can this be?" he asked, his eyes growing wide. "I have seen my dead ancestors at the feast day celebrations and have danced in honor of our departed ones. They appear above the flames of the fire when we worship the spirits at our dances."

"They are not your ancestors, I assure you," Pastor Silsbee said gravely. "They are demonic spirits that perform signs and wonders. 'We do not wrestle against flesh and blood, but against principalities, against powers, against the rulers of the darkness of this age, against spiritual hosts of wickedness in the heavenly places' [Ephesians 6:12, NKJV].

"As for your departed loved ones, Thomas, the Bible says, 'the living know that they will die; but the dead know nothing' [Ecclesiastes 9:5, NKJV]. When their spirits depart, they return to the ground; on that very day their plans come to nothing [see Psalm 146:4]."

Thomas seemed very concerned on hearing such a new concept, but then a look of peace and tranquility came over his face. "Actually, this is very good news for me," he said quietly. "All of my life I have feared the power of the evil spirits. I have feared the witch doctor who can be paid to put a curse on anyone who displeases him.

"But I have worried myself sick about upsetting the good spirits too. This is the part of my culture I do not like. If a loved family member dies and I do not pay proper respect to him or her at the funeral, there will be trouble for me. I have always feared the day when I must die and enter the boat that will cross the ocean of death. When I reach the other side to begin the afterlife, all those relatives that I did not treat well in death will push my boat back out to sea, and there I will drift for eternity."

Pastor Silsbee listened respectfully until Thomas had finished. "These are common stories from many African tribes," he replied, "and I can understand your fears. But let me assure you, Thomas, you need not worry about any of the spirits, either bad or good. All such spirits that make you afraid are the spirits of devils, and they are working day and night against the kingdom of God. Listen to this passage. 'Our struggle is not against flesh and blood, but against the rulers, against the authorities, against the powers of this dark world and against the spiritual forces of evil in the heavenly realms' [Ephesians 6:12, NIV]."

The moon had come up by now, appearing from time to time as it passed through the branches of a baobab tree outside the open window. By now, Pastor Silsbee had lit a lantern so they could continue reading their Bibles. The flickering flames cast shadows that jumped and danced on the whitewashed wall of the missionary's mud-brick home.

And on they talked. The rest of Pastor Silsbee's family went to bed, but the two men remained at the table, absorbed in their study. Thomas was as thirsty for the Word of God as if he were in a desert without water. When they finally stopped hours later, it was well after midnight, and Thomas apologized for keeping Pastor Silsbee up.

"No need for apologies," Pastor Silsbee assured him. "There are times in life when we just cannot go to bed because we are making new discoveries in the Word of God. Jesus Himself sometimes stayed awake all night praying, you know."

Thomas grinned tiredly. "Well, I surely don't want to keep you up all night. I know I'd overstay my welcome if I got that carried away."

In the days that followed, Pastor Silsbee continued teaching Thomas Bible truths. Thomas learned many new things, and many of the ideas surprised him almost as much as the truth about the Sabbath. He learned about paying a faithful tithe of all he earned and about baptism by immersion as Jesus was baptized.

They studied about the soon coming of Jesus too. " 'Every eye will see Him,' " Pastor Silsbee told Thomas. " 'As lightning that comes from the east is visible even in the west, so will be the coming of the Son of Man' [Revelation 1:7, NKJV; Matthew 24:27, NIV]."

Thomas stayed with Pastor Silsbee at the mission for several weeks. They studied and prayed together, ate together, and worked in the mission gardens. He listened to the missionary teach the young men in the school how to give Bible studies. He listened as Pastor Silsbee preached about God's remnant people to the villagers who came to worship at Sabbath services.

That God has a remnant people who live near the end of time especially interested Thomas. "Is it true that I am one of God's chosen people?" he asked. "Is it true that He has a special work for me to do?"

"That's what the Bible says," Pastor Silsbee replied. "Jesus' instruction to His disciples was, 'Go and make disciples of all nations, baptizing them in the name of the Father and of the Son and of the Holy Spirit, and teaching them to obey everything I have commanded you. And surely I am with you always, to the very end of the age' [Matthew 28:19, 20, NIV]."

Thomas thought about that and finally said, "Then I must be a missionary for God as you are."

"Wonderful," Pastor Silsbee agreed, "and I think you're ready. But now there is one more thing you need to do before you go."

Thomas smiled. "I know, I know, I must be baptized."

And so it was that the missionary pastor baptized Thomas one Sabbath morning in the river that ran beside the mission property.

Church members sang as Thomas disappeared beneath the water, and the angels of heaven sang as he walked out of the river, a new man with a new commission from God.

"And now I must be moving on," Thomas said, beaming with happiness. "It's time for me to begin my first missionary journey."

"I think this is number two for you." Pastor Silsbee laughed. "Your trip up here to find the mission was your first."

Thomas grinned. "This is true, but I didn't know a tenth then of what I know now."

Pastor Silsbee shook his head. "God uses us all when we are ready and willing, not by how educated we are."

Part 4: Paralytic to Evangelist

The day Thomas left the mission everyone came to see him off. Pastor Silsbee's family prayed with him and shed a few tears. In the few weeks he had been with them, they had grown to love him as one of their family. The boys in the school came to shake his hand, and the elders in the church gave him their blessing. Even the young Bible workers in training took time off to say Goodbye.

Thomas gave them all a promise that he would come again to see them when he was back that way on one of his missionary journeys.

His goal on this first trip for Jesus was to work his way back to his home village. No one was more on his mind than his own people. "They are a tribe in total darkness, for no one is so blind as those who will not see," he kept saying to himself.

And so he started out, working his way back east the way he had come, stopping to visit those he had challenged with his testimony on the way to the mission. Many ridiculed him as they had before, but some listened to his message of the Sabbath and the soon coming of Jesus. In some places, where he found interest, he stayed for a few weeks to instruct the people about the Bible teachings that had changed his life so completely. The Sabbath came to be very special to these dear ones, and so was his message that they need not fear the evil spirits anymore.

"God is infinitely more powerful than the spiritual forces of darkness," Thomas told them, and it was wonderful to see the changes that came over the villagers when they accepted this new truth by faith.

In these remote places, Thomas raised up companies of believers and appointed leaders who could direct the work of sharing the three angels' messages in the infant churches. It was a difficult thing he was doing—a challenge with almost impossible odds. After he left, how could he expect these people to continue worshiping as he had instructed them in the short time he was with them? How could he expect them to maintain their beliefs, when they were all so young in the faith? But then he remembered his own story and how quickly he had grown in understanding the Bible through the strength and nurturing of the Lord.

Not surprisingly, it was the message of Jesus' soon coming that made the biggest difference in the lives of these small companies of believers. "We will see each other again when Jesus comes in the clouds of heaven," Thomas would tell them all confidently, and it was with tears that they would send him away to the next stop on his missionary journey.

All along the roadway from the Kolo Mission Station back to Mafeking, Thomas stopped at every village, no matter how small, no matter what the reception. If the people welcomed him, he stayed for a while. If they shouted him out of town, he shook the dust from his sandals and went on to "greener pastures," as Jesus had instructed His disciples.

When he finally reached his own home village, the people came out to meet him. By now, his reputation as a missionary traveler had spread far and wide, preceding him on his journey. Many of those who had laughed before welcomed him now.

The old witch doctor resisted the message Thomas brought, but he soon saw it was pointless to work against the son of the great Chief Kabelo.

However, when the people asked Thomas to stay and become their chief as old Kabelo had wanted, Thomas kindly turned them down. "I cannot," he said with conviction. "I must be on my way to spread the light of the three angels' messages to others who have not heard it. Jesus is coming soon to take to heaven those who want an eternal home, and I must help them get ready. Fear not the work of Satan among you, for he is far weaker than our Father in heaven. And remember to keep the Sabbath day holy. 'Six days you shall labor . . . but the seventh day is the Sabbath of the LORD your God. In it you shall do no work' [Exodus 20:9, 10, NKJV]."

And then he moved on. For years, he traveled among the villages of Basutoland, telling the good news of the gospel. Nothing was heard from him for quite some time, and then news finally reached Pastor Silsbee at the Kolo Mission Station that Thomas had died in the influenza epidemic of 1919.

At first no one would believe it, for Thomas had been one of the strongest and healthiest among them since he had been miraculously healed. He had been a faithful missionary, made many friends, and had great success among the tribes of people along the border of British Bechuanaland and the Transvaal region east of Mafeking.

But further inquiries and a trip to Lokaleng, where Thomas had spent his last days, confirmed their worst fears. Thomas Sehare had indeed fallen in the line of duty.

In 1920, when Elder William Anderson came looking for a place to plant a mission in Bechuanaland, he made a happy discovery. Brother Thomas had died in the service of his Master, but his witness lived on. All along the road from the Kolo Mission Station to Mafeking was found a string of villages with Sabbath keepers in them.

Many tears were shed by the folks who lived in this region when they told the story of how Thomas had shared with them the three angels' messages. There is no record of Thomas's final message to the companies of believers he left behind, and only the angels know how many souls he won for the kingdom. But we can thank God today that Thomas wanted to be a missionary to spread the gospel. When Jesus comes again, Thomas will awake to receive his crown of righteousness.

Kiss the Ring

Part 1: The Mayor Frees Akim

The year was 1917. The Great War was being fought, and no one could predict the end of this "war to end all wars." Day after day the stories from both sides of the conflict filled the newspapers, each attempting to paint a good picture of its side. But the reality of war could not be disguised.

Every factory in Europe, it seemed, had been retooled to produce weapons and war supplies. In countries such as Romania, military losses climbed astronomically. More than two hundred thousand Romanian soldiers had died in the war, leaving their families to struggle with grief and poverty.

The Romanian government had been allied with the Russians against the Austro-Hungarian armies and had been turning out recruits for service on the eastern front, but this was becoming more difficult. People were tired of the war and no longer wanted to send their men to support it.

But the politicians who had started the war were determined to win, and anyone who failed to give full cooperation was blacklisted. Romania's minister of war, a staunch atheist, was one such politician who considered winning worth any human cost.

When he heard that many Seventh-day Adventist men would not carry guns in the military and that they requested to be excused from duty on Sabbath, he took swift action. First, he ordered officers to punish every Adventist soldier who would not cooperate with his superiors. As a result, every military camp in the country adopted harsh measures against the Seventh-day Adventists who had standards about when and how they would serve.

In one case, a Romanian medical student named Peter Paulini was drafted to serve in the Romanian army, but he would not agree to carry a gun or work on Sabbath. The sergeant of his platoon became very angry and sent him to the commanding officer at headquarters.

"You'll do time in the military stockade if I have anything to say about it!" the sergeant snarled.

But Peter would not be intimidated and, surprisingly, was rewarded for his faithfulness. When he arrived at headquarters, he discovered the commanding officer was a long-lost friend.

When Peter's unit was moved to a new army camp six weeks later, he encountered the same problem; and wonder of wonders, this time the commanding officer was a college classmate. Each time this happened, he was allowed special consideration and was excused from regular military duty on the Sabbath.

Doing office work or performing medical duties might seem like mundane work to some soldiers, but Peter was willing to perform such tasks if he would be allowed to honor the Sabbath. Even cleaning horse stalls was not considered beneath his dignity. And best of all, during this time, he was given the freedom to share the gospel with anyone he chose. As a result, scores of recruits and officers in the army learned of God's saving grace.

Unfortunately, persecution within the military had a way of trickling down to the civilian population. The state church was envious of Seventh-day Adventists because of their success rate in evangelism. When the bishops and priests saw the negative attention Seventh-day Adventists were receiving in the military, they decided to take advantage of it. To them, it seemed the perfect opportunity to rid their country of Protestant influences. Many members of the state church had high government positions that they could use to enforce the restrictions.

And so it was that the minister of war, in cooperation with the state church, gave an order that every civilian employee must abandon his or her Seventh-day Adventist beliefs and join the state church—or be fired. Dozens of Adventists lost their jobs under this new law, and what a trial it became for them.

Another oppressive law decreed that when a bishop came to mass or a public meeting, everyone must kneel and kiss the cross in his ring as he passed by. If anyone should refuse to kneel, the new law allowed for the bishop's bodyguard to form a line, file past the guilty one, and spit on that person. Many questioned God's leading in this time of distress, but many more Adventists praised His name that they could suffer for the sake of the gospel. After all, Jesus Himself had been abused and spit upon for their sakes.

And, as if this were not enough, the minister of education soon announced that all Protestant parents of school-aged children would be imprisoned if they did not send their children to the state-run Catholic schools. Adventist families everywhere were terrified at this new edict. If their children were taken away from them, what would prevent the little ones from being forced to give up their faith?

But they needn't have worried, for God had a plan and sent His angels to give the children courage and wisdom in their greatest time of need. Though many families went into hiding at this time to avoid the confiscation of their children, some were caught, and their children promptly taken to the state schools. In this way, many families were given opportunities to witness for their faith.

In one town, Akim, a fifteen-year-old boy, was taken to a Catholic school where he was told they "would get the Adventist religion out of him" and make him a Catholic for sure. However, after whipping him and depriving him of food for days, they found him all the more determined to be faithful to his Adventist beliefs.

"You can kill me," Akim said bravely, "but I will never disobey my Savior whom my mother taught me to love." When the local mayor heard of the mistreatment, he ordered the boy set free.

Soon most of the church members had gone underground, and the members were suffering much hardship. Many had no place to live because their property had been taken. Denied jobs, they could not earn a living. Still the Seventh-day Adventists remained faithful in winning souls for the kingdom. And though they were often brought to trial before the authorities, they rejoiced that they could suffer for Jesus, who had suffered so much for them.

But the devil would not let God's people rest. When the state church realized it could not break the spirit of Seventh-day Adventism in Romania, it made one final attempt to eliminate the proclamation of the three angels' messages from the land.

The minister of the interior now ordered police in every province of Romania to arrest all Adventist pastors, teachers, and Bible workers, and deliver them to the government. Some were easy to find because they owned businesses; but to capture others, they had to rely on trickery. In some cases, policemen masqueraded as potential converts to the church. They set up sting operations to find out the secret places where Adventists worshiped and then promptly had them arrested.

In the city of Galati, the persecution was especially severe; many believers were thrown into jail until more than one hundred Adventists were awaiting trial. When the local officials felt they had corralled most of the Adventists, a day was set for a hearing.

On the morning of the hearing, the Adventist prisoners were taken to a local Seventh-day Adventist church that the government had confiscated, and were told to sit in the pews until the district bishop arrived.

Not surprisingly, an unruly mob of several hundred people began to gather outside the church, obviously part of the overall plan. Everyone knew it was a common practice for the local priests to collect a gang of ruffians on a morning like this and then get them drunk at a local pub. It was a perfect way to bait a crowd. After that, the rest was easy.

For several hours, everyone waited. When the old bishop finally arrived, what a show his entrance made. His robes of scarlet velvet shimmered when he stepped down from his carriage drawn by four white horses. His golden crosier sparkled as he walked grandly to the door of the Seventh-day Adventist church. A red carpet had been rolled up the steps to the church by his retinue of priests, and he paused momentarily to allow those kneeling nearest him to kiss his ring as he passed.

At that moment, the mayor also arrived, and with him were more than fifty soldiers, their long sabers rattling in scabbards at their sides. The boisterous crowd parted to let the soldiers through, but they hissed and hooted at them as they passed. About half of the soldiers formed a barricade around the church, while the others filed inside or stood guard on the church steps.

Part 2: Cosmina Speaks Up

The church was crowded as the bishop and mayor entered, but none of the Adventists dared lift their heads as the two passed. They had been through so much, and it looked like worse persecution was to come. Most of the stalwart leaders from their past were gone now. Some had been sent to prisons far away as an example to those who might dare to stand in their place. Some had died because of the hardships imposed on them.

From outward appearances, the church in Galati would be eliminated. The Adventists would probably be coerced into signing a proclamation that forbade them from using the Seventh-day Adventist name in Romania again. They would be declared enemies of the state and would likely be banished. It was no surprise that the group of Adventists was being arraigned before a state-church court to decide on their guilt and punishment.

And the real question of the day was, What exactly were the charges? Was it that they loved God? Was it that they did not want to give up the Seventh-day Adventist teachings and values they held so dear? Or was it that they wouldn't kiss the bishop's ring?

A small lectern, inlaid with gold and ivory, had been placed on the platform from which the bishop would speak, and the seat cushion of the bishop's chair matched his scarlet robes perfectly.

After a few minutes of waiting, the stately old bishop stood to address the captive group of Adventists. With his intimidating bearing, he frowned down at the Adventists as if he were their schoolmaster and they were naughty pupils. "I'm sure you all know why you have been brought here," he announced coldly. "To honor the church should be the highest goal of any child of God, but this you have not done. You have blasphemed the Lord's name by preaching heresies that do not agree with the mother church. Shame be to you and all your kind! God's curse is upon you for not submitting to the decrees of the state church."

The bishop continued the accusation, condemning the Seventh-day Adventist congregation for their strange beliefs and their lack of "common sense" when it came to spiritual truths. It was clear that he was hoping to bully them into submission to his authority.

"This town has no place for heretics like you," he continued, "and the only thing for you to do now is leave. You are lost souls, every one of you. As bishop of God's church and the highest religious authority in Galati, I therefore excommunicate you forever from the mother church. I condemn your souls to the eternal flames of purgatory when this mortal life shall pass, until such a time that God may have mercy upon your souls."

His words would have been very disturbing to the average citizen of Galati, for they all revered the state church and the authority the church claimed it had over heaven and hell. But to Adventists, the excommunication itself wasn't particularly frightening. Every Seventh-day Adventist was a Bible student and knew there was no basis for any claims that the bishop might have about heresy, excommunication, and the fires of purgatory.

Most of the members still sat with eyes averted as the bishop ranted, but a few looked around. They noticed that the mayor, who was seated on the platform behind the bishop, kept nodding off sleepily—the only light moment of the morning. The soldiers lining the walls of the church sanctuary tried to hide their smiles, but it was difficult, especially when the mayor's head repeatedly jerked forward, awakening him with a start.

The Adventists could hear the increasing noise of the crowd outside. What would happen next? they wondered. Were enough soldiers present to keep the crowd under control? One look out of the church windows told them the task might not be easy.

But the bishop wasn't finished yet. "I must say I feel a certain sense of responsibility for this group of heretics," he added, pretending to be benevolent. "If it pleases the Almighty Lord God, I wish to extend one last offer of mercy for those who will avail themselves of the opportunity. If you will agree to come forward now to kneel at my feet, kiss this ring, and confess your heresies, it may be that we can pray for a lesser punishment in the fires of hell." He glanced around at the faces below him. "By the authority invested in me as high bishop of Galati and representative of God and the mother church, I will do my best to plead your case before the Mother Mary to shorten your stay in purgatory."

No one moved. Then, as the bishop's voice took on a kinder tone, the Adventists, one by one, lifted their heads to stare up at him. He had now come out from behind the lectern and walked a few steps closer to the people.

Finally, one man stood hesitantly to his feet and went forward. Soon others stood and followed him.

The old bishop tried not to show his delight at having gained such a compromise from the Adventists, but it was evident he had triumphed. Soon they were all going forward and kneeling before the bishop. All, that is, except Cosmina, a little woman who still sat on the back row of the church. In dismay, she watched her brothers and sisters kneeling before the bishop, but finally she could stand it no longer. She jumped to her feet and shouted, "This man is not God! Are we going to pray to a bishop? We have been taught to bow only to God."

Cosmina sprang to the side of her husband, one of the first to have gone forward. "In the name of Jesus, I ask you to stand to your feet," she begged.

"All of you!" she called, looking at her Adventist friends. "Choose for yourselves this day whom you will serve."

The mayor was wide awake now, and the soldiers were on full alert. The bishop himself was stunned as all the Adventists members slowly stood to their feet and moved back toward their seats. His eyes darted back and forth across the congregation, and his white mustache twitched nervously.

And then something happened that proved beyond a doubt that Satan himself was present at the meeting. As the news of what was happening inside spread to the mob outside, the ruffians began shouting and cursing. "Kill the woman! Kill the woman!" they chanted in a demonic tone that sent shivers down the spine of every person inside the church.

Even the mayor was disturbed by what he was hearing. As the roar of the crowd grew louder, the windows in the church seemed to rattle.

The soldiers gripped their swords as they glanced out the windows, and the Adventist members began to huddle together.

Suddenly, the commanding officer strode down the center aisle of the church. "Take your swords!" he commanded his soldiers, as he drew his own sword from its scabbard. "Everyone take an Adventist by the hand. I'll take the little woman myself," he said, pointing at Cosmina.

At this, all the Adventists pulled back in fear. Was this how it would end for them? They had shamed their Lord by denying Him as the apostle Peter had done so long ago, and now they must pay the price for it! Would the soldiers kill them here and now? It seemed so, and many of the women began to weep hysterically.

The mayor stood to his feet, dumbfounded at this turn of events. The bishop, though startled, had now regained his composure and seemed almost gratified. If the Adventists would not use good judgment and submit to his authority, then perhaps they should pay with their lives, he reasoned.

But then the commanding officer surprised them all with startling words that put everyone in their place. Turning to the mayor, he said, "You have a duty to protect the weak. Do it!"

And to the bishop, he simply said, "You, most honorable bishop, were sent to preach the gospel. Stick to your commission!"

Then he glanced around the church sanctuary and quickly added, "Men at arms! Clear a path to the door and lead the Adventists home. If anyone here ever molests the Adventists again, they will have to answer to me."

At this, the mayor and his soldiers opened the church doors, parted the crowd, and escorted all the Adventists to safety.

And so it was that God protected Adventist believers yet again. The worst that Satan had managed to muster against the Adventists had amounted to nothing in the face of God's almighty power. Truly, "the eyes of the Lord are on the righteous, and his ears are attentive to their cry" (Psalm 34:15, NIV).

Never Too Old

Part 1: Send Me

In 1882, a small Seventh-day Adventist congregation was started among the German immigrants in Milltown, South Dakota. The three angels' messages had been brought to the Dakotas by Elder Louis Conradi, who was himself of German-Russian descent. Copying his missionary spirit, the members of the little church began sending Bible tracts to the Crimea in southern Russia. Naturally, they wanted to share the excitement of their newfound faith with family and friends in the old country.

Later, when letters began arriving from relatives in Russia saying that some had accepted the Bible truths they had read in the tracts, the South Dakota Adventists were very excited. "God has blessed us for our missionary efforts," the head elder said with conviction. "What we really need to do is to send someone to the Crimea as a missionary to teach the people about the Bible truths we have learned. That way they would hear the entire gospel."

But whom could they send? Most of the South Dakota farmers had arrived fairly recently, and had staked claims on quarter sections of farmland. If they left before they fulfilled their mandatory five-year commitment to the land, they would lose their deeds to the property.

They thought of sending a petition to the General Conference, asking them to send a missionary to the Crimea, but that might take years. They didn't want to wait! The challenge of sharing the three angels' messages, to which they had been converted, was still fresh in their minds, and they believed that Jesus was coming soon. Loved ones back in Russia were dying with no knowledge of salvation, the coming judgment, or life after death. How could they not send a missionary?

One evening, the church called a meeting to discuss how they might select someone to send as missionary to the Crimea. Everyone was at the meeting, and the pastor was doing his best to lead the discussion. First, one solution was offered and then another, but no one seemed able to agree on any plan.

Finally, Philipp Reiswig, one of the oldest members who had been an Adventist for about five years, stood to his feet. "I th-th-think the biggest problem in our church is th-th-that we all want to send a missionary," he stuttered in his characteristic way, "but unfortunately, n-n-none of us wants to be th-th-that missionary."

"Well now, that's not quite fair," the pastor replied, smiling at Philipp's efforts to express himself. "We are all doing our best to be a light in this farming community. Not everyone can go as a missionary, you know."

"What y-y-you say is true, but we are not t-t-talking about everyone here," Philipp replied to the pastor. "We are talking about j-j-just one. All w-w-we need is just o-o-one missionary to go to the Crimea. One, and I have not s-s-seen that one person standing up and offering to go."

At this comment, everyone in the meeting grew quiet. Not a word was spoken as they all sat thinking about the wisdom of Philipp's words.

The old man's eyes ranged across the congregation of his fellow believers, but still no one said anything. Finally, he stepped out from the wooden pew and into the aisle. "I'll g-g-go," he said simply. "N-N-No names have been sent to us from B-B-Battle Creek, and none of us h-h-here in this church is willing to go."

"You?" the pastor asked, his eyes big with surprise.

"Yes, me!" Philipp pulled himself up to his full height of five-feet, six-inches. "I'm as s-s-strong as an ox! As f-f-fit as the day I came here about eight years ago with my wife and daughter to homestead here in South Dakota."

"How old are you, Brother Philipp?" the pastor asked kindly, not wanting to overemphasize the point.

"In my sixties."

"In your sixties?"

"That's right, s-s-sir. W-W-Why do you ask?"

The pastor stared at Philipp. "I think you know why," the pastor stated.

"Oh, I suppose y-y-you think I'm too old to go to the Crimea!" Philipp felt indignant, but he tried not to show it.

"Well, yes, and I'm sure there are many here who would say the same thing. You're a good man, Brother Philipp. You've lived a full life, and you're a man of God. But that doesn't mean you need to travel to the far corners of the earth to be a missionary. There's much you can do right here at home."

"But I w-w-want to go to the Crimea," Philipp blushed a little. He was beginning to sound like a little boy now.

There was silence again for a few moments, and then the pastor finally regained his composure. "It's late, folks. I think we'd better head home now. We'll discuss this some more next week."

Philipp wasn't present at the next meeting, and many in the room now felt more free to express themselves. "He's too old to travel so far," they said impatiently.

"He's too feeble," others added. "He'll never hold up to the rigors of being a missionary."

"He has poor eyesight, and besides that, he stutters something fierce," a young farmer exclaimed. "I work with him, and some days I can hardly understand what he's trying to say."

They all half-smiled, knowing Philipp's stuttering was perhaps his worst enemy. How could he share the gospel with complete strangers when the first thing they heard would be his speech defect? He was a godly old soul; but in their minds there was just too much working against him to let him go off to the Crimea. "You can't take an old man seriously who doesn't know his own shortcomings," they all agreed.

But Philipp would hear none of it. "I've m-m-made up my mind," he announced two Sabbaths later in church. "I'll g-g-give you a month to find someone else, but if you haven't f-f-found a man to do the job by then, I'm g-g-going."

No one could talk him out of it. Trying to reason with him was like trying to convince a dog it doesn't need a bone. "You are the most stubborn man I've ever known," the pastor told him.

Philipp's wife had died, so he didn't need to worry about providing for her. And so, as a last resort, the church finally agreed to let him go, not that they could have prevented it. But they did send him away with their blessing, a wooden crate of Bible tracts printed in German, and a rucksack full of their best German baked goods.

Part 2: Exhausting Voyage

The trip did prove to be difficult for a man of Philipp's age, not that he was surprised. He had known the journey would be hard and tiring, but he didn't care. He wanted to serve God, and he felt a conviction that God needed him in the Crimea, especially since no one from his home congregation had offered to go. Then, too, there was something in him that rose to the challenge, not letting him settle for the idea that he was too old to be a missionary.

Traveling conditions were a trial. He planned to buy a train ticket to the East Coast but was unwilling to pay the six dollars it would cost, so he arranged to ride in the mail coach, eating his own meals and sleeping on the mail bags. He had to pass through Chicago, Cleveland, and New York City to get to the port where his ship would embark, and he was afraid to leave the train, for fear he might lose his place in the mail car.

Once before he had made such a trip from the Crimea to the United States, and he remembered the trip vividly, as if it were only yesterday.

But now things were different. Philipp was returning from the Land of Promise to the place of his birth. Not to a land of bondage, as some might call it, where wars plagued the land, and the government cared little for common folks. He was going back to share the gospel, armed with the Word of God to instruct those who wished to be heirs of salvation. And he had his precious crate of religious tracts.

Springtime had come to the Dakota prairies, and he enjoyed watching the slowly passing landscape as he traveled. He loved this time of year when nature was bursting with life and vitality. The green prairie stretched as far as the eye could see, and farmers were breaking new ground.

The train chugged across the prairie, giving Philipp a chance to think about his one last mission in life. "I'm going to make it as a missionary if it's the last thing I do," he kept telling himself. "I'll pitch my tent like Abraham, if I need to. I'm just a pilgrim here, looking for a city 'whose builder and maker is God' [Hebrews 11:10, NKJV]."

The baked goods the church members had sent with him lasted the entire journey from the Dakotas to New York City, and he even had some to spare for the ocean voyage. By the time he ate the last loaf of bread, it was quite hard, and the pastries were stale, but he didn't mind. "I've lived on old cabbage and rutabagas many a year when the spring came late, and the gardens had to wait to be planted," he reminded himself.

At the docks in New York City, he arranged to get passage on a cargo steamer. It was heading for Europe in just a few hours, and he counted himself blessed for the timely connection. Shipping docks were not the best place to be while waiting for passage, and he prayed that God would keep him in the care of His angels.

"Ah, what would anyone want with an old man, anyway?" Philipp joked to himself. "I've got only a few dollars. If a hoodlum wants some of my religious tracts, I'll gladly share 'em. Might do him some good." He had to laugh at the thought of giving a bandit a Bible study.

As the ship steamed out of port late that afternoon, Philipp turned his back on the city that had first greeted him so many years before. The endless ocean stretched away to the east and to the gray-green horizon beyond. Leaving everything behind gave him a strange feeling, and he even shed a tear or two.

"Heaven is my home now," Philipp told himself, acknowledging that he would not be making the return journey.

The ship on which he sailed was not a typical boat for common travelers. There were no quarters for passengers, and Philipp slept in a boiler room in a hammock strung from the ceiling.

The trip went well the first day out; but on the second day, a stiff wind came up, and the swells grew deep and long. Within a few hours, Philipp was as sick as he ever remembered being in his life. It was embarrassing for him, for he was a man of German stock and prided himself on his sturdy constitution. He hated standing at the rail, with his head over the side of the ship, but what else could he do? The rise and fall of the ship would not let his stomach rest. "I don't remember it being this bad the first time I made the voyage," he mumbled as he watched the green waves of ocean spray hit the bow of the ship.

Finally, he retired to his hammock with a wooden bucket, determined he would stay there until his body adjusted to the motion. He prayed that God would help him make it through the voyage.

But worse was to come. The very next day a storm hit, and soon Philipp's hammock swayed mercilessly. For two days, the storm raged; and all the while Philipp could not eat, of course. By the time the storm finally subsided, he was pale, weak, and unsteady on his legs.

The ship's captain saw him staggering along the deck the next morning, trying to keep his balance against the rail, and took pity on him. "What have you got to eat?" he asked.

"Not a lot," Philipp admitted. "But I'll be all right, sir."

The captain grinned from behind the tobacco pipe he held tight in his teeth. "Well, you're a brave one, old-timer," he said with a grunt. "When you feel like you're ready to eat, come by the galley, and I'll see that you get some real food. You can help the cook prepare meals for the crew in payment for what you eat," he added, when he saw the look of protest on Philipp's face.

Things got better for Philipp after the captain's kind offer, and he finally did get his sea legs back.

When he reached Europe a few days later, Philipp boarded a train that was on its way to Odessa. By now his money had run out, and he had nothing left to pay for his fare to the Crimea. He was a stranger without a penny to his name, and no one to care whether he reached his destination or not. He even thought of begging, but his German pride would not let him do this.

Finally, he decided to sell his good leather boots, the only thing he had left of value, and with this money he paid for his ticket. He would not part with his precious Bible tracts, for with those he must evangelize the Crimea.

Part 3: "Can You R-R-Read It for Me?"

Philipp's greatest challenge now was to find a place to stay, and he found one near the open market. By God's direction, he chanced to meet Aleksander, whom he had known years before in their home village, when they were much younger.

They had last seen each other following the Crimean War. Later Philipp and his wife had gone to America. Aleksander had stayed in the home country, where he was a cobbler, still making and repairing shoes in the marketplace.

Aleksander was so happy to see Philipp again after all these years that he offered him a place to sleep on the balcony of his one-room flat. He would give this in exchange for help in preparing the leather he used for making shoes. New hides needed to be scraped and cured with oil to prepare them properly for making shoes.

And so by night Philipp worked in leather, but by day he set out to fulfill his dream. "I d-d-didn't come all the way from S-S-South Dakota just to make s-s-shoes," he told Aleksander. "I c-c-came to tell others the g-g-good news of the three angels' messages." The two of them laughed together at the sight of the elderly man buttoning on his suspenders that first morning.

In the marketplace, Philipp set about to find a good method of sharing the gospel. He could just hand out the Bible tracts, but most people on the streets did not seem interested in what he had to say. Many would take the tract when he handed it to them and look at it briefly, but he got the idea that they were more interested in the value of the paper than they were in the spiritual message it contained. He didn't want to believe it, but he knew it was true because sometimes he would see a customer in the market walking by with a loaf of bread or a piece of meat wrapped in one of his Bible tracts.

He knew he shouldn't let it bother him, but it did. Information about the precious Word of God was being used merely for wrapping food. Then, again, he reasoned that God could do whatever He wanted with the tracts. If He wanted to send His tracts abroad in the form of market wrappings, then that was His business.

And then Philipp thought of another plan. Maybe he could read the tracts publicly to people in the streets as if he were an evangelist on a street corner. He tried that; but the people didn't seem interested when he read, and no one stopped to listen. Probably they were too busy, or maybe they just thought he was a strange old man stuttering to himself.

And then one day, he forgot his reading glasses and couldn't really see well enough to read to the folks as they passed. What should he do? He could go back to the house to get them, but that would take time. Then he saw a young man coming down the street who looked nice enough to approach, and the impression came to him that he should ask the young man to read to him.

"E-E-Excuse me, s-s-sir," Philipp said as he stepped out in front of the young man and extended the tract to him. "I was w-w-wondering if you m-m-might be able to help me? I have this little t-t-tract here, but I left my r-r-reading glasses at home and c-c-can't read it. Can you r-r-read it for me, and tell me w-w-what it says?"

The young man glanced at him in pity for a moment, and then took the paper. He scanned the tract quickly. "OK. Which part shall I read?"

"I was l-l-looking at this part here," Philipp said, pointing to the second column, which happened to be on the subject of Jesus' soon coming.

"All right," the young man replied. "Let's see. It says Jesus' coming will not be in secret, but it will be a surprise to those who are unprepared. Then it says, 'The

Lord Himself will descend from heaven with a shout, with the voice of an archangel, and with the trumpet of God. And the dead in Christ will rise first' [1 Thessalonians 4:16, NKJV]. 'We shall not all sleep, but we shall all be changed—in a moment, in the twinkling of an eye, at the last trumpet. For the trumpet will sound, and the dead will be raised incorruptible, and we shall be changed' [1 Corinthians 15:51, 52, NKJV]."

"Oh, I like t-t-that." Philipp smiled. "C-C-Can't you just see it?" As the young man tried to hand the tract back to him, Philipp quickly added, "Please, sir, if you don't mind, could you read just one more part for me? I do so like to hear the Word of God. Would you, please?"

The young man glanced at Philipp again, hesitated, and then finally nodded. "OK, which part now?"

"T-T-This one here." Philipp smiled again and closed his eyes in enjoyment.

"The resurrected believers are caught up to meet their Lord in the air," the young man continued reading. "Angels gather God's people from all around the world. Little children are carried by holy angels to their mothers' arms. Friends long separated by death are reunited, nevermore to part, and with songs of gladness they ascend together to the City of God."

"Oh t-t-that's grand," Philipp exclaimed excitely. "I just l-l-love that part! I can hardly w-w-wait for that day!"

And then as the young man tried again to hand back the tract, Philipp simply said, "Oh, that's all right. You can keep it for all the help you've given me."

And now it was the young man's turn to smile. "Thank you very much," he said. "This does sound rather interesting, I have to admit. I think I'll finish reading it when I get home tonight," and with that he was gone.

Philipp was excited as he watched the young man go, knowing that a precious seed had been sown. And his own need had been the beginning of his opportunity to witness. But the strangest thing about the whole routine was that something so simple could work so well.

After that, Philipp left his reading glasses home every day and established a morning routine at the market. Because he could not see well, he would step up to a stranger walking by in the street and ask him or her to read part of a tract for him. If he liked what he heard, he would make some comment, and then ask the person to read a little more. When the stranger had finished reading the tract, Philipp would tell the person to keep the tract for his or her kindness to an old man.

Not surprisingly, God blessed Philipp's efforts at witnessing. Soon there were groups of Sabbath keepers springing up in several of the small towns and villages in the Crimea. No Seventh-day Adventist pastors worked in the area at that time, so Philipp did his best to make his rounds and preach in his limited way. After all, he was well into his sixties by now.

The local priests of the Russian Orthodox Church grew increasingly angry at the old man's success. "Who invited that troublemaker here?" they wanted to know. "Who does he think he is—stirring up the people on religious doctrines that don't concern them! We've worked hard to bring them religion. We don't need some old man getting in the way. He's got to go!"

"But he's only an old man," the town councilors would protest. "How much harm can an old man do?" And the priests were forced to leave him alone.

And so the three angels' messages began to reach people in the Crimea, and souls were won for the kingdom of God because an old man refused to listen to those who had no faith in his ability to share the three angels' messages. Someday soon, when Jesus comes, old Philipp will find out just how effective his adventures as a missionary were. For now, it should encourage us all to do our parts in sharing the love of Jesus with others. It doesn't matter whether we are old or young, large or small, rich or poor. Jesus can use us no matter who we are.

Wings of a Dove

Part 1: Dakila's Dream

Crisanto couldn't sleep. He tossed and turned, but the blessed relief of sleep would not come. Crickets chirped and an owl screeched from somewhere outside the window of his bungalow. Every little sound, it seemed, jarred his nerves, keeping him awake. *It must be close to dawn,* he thought, as he got up once again to get a drink of water from the water bucket in the kitchen.

The old clock on the wall showed 9:10 A.M., as it had all of these years since it had broken. The clock had been given to him and his wife on their wedding day some twenty-three years earlier, the most valuable gift they had received, but it broke sometime during the years that followed. He didn't even know when, but the old clock seemed symbolic somehow of his own life—broken and pointless, stuck at 9:10 A.M.

What did Crisanto have in life that had purpose? He was a pastor of eight small Methodist congregations in Natonin and the surrounding villages of the northern Luzon Island in the Philippines; but ever since his little girl, Imee, had died, that no longer seemed enough. And how long had that been? He had lost track of that, too, but he guessed it must be more than ten years now.

Imee had been the joy of their lives—the most delightful of children—always happy and cheerful. They would hear her singing her little songs from Sunday School when she was swinging on the rope Crisanto had hung for her in the old mango tree. And she loved all the little creatures that lived in the forest around their home. Every day she came in with some little bug, lizard, or other tiny creature. The creatures did not seem afraid of her, for she was gentle and spoke kind words to them, petting the little animals as if they were her own little children.

She was the only child Amihan could conceive, and it had cut like knives the day they had laid her in the grave in the little cemetery outside of Natonin. She had died of a disease they called influenza. Others had gotten the disease and had recovered, but it proved to be too much for Imee. Crisanto had not admitted it to anyone, but his faith in God had diminished much since that day. How could a loving God allow little Imee to die when she had so much of life yet to live? The questions remained unanswered for Crisanto.

Crisanto went back to the bed and lay down beside Amihan. She did not stir; he watched her face for several long minutes, still lovely, but careworn after all of these years. How she had made it through the trying ordeal of their daughter's loss, he could not imagine. She was spiritually stronger than he was, though folks in their congregations didn't know it.

He tried to go back to sleep but could not. The ceiling seemed so far away as he lay on his back staring up at it. That was a strange feeling to have in the middle of the night, but it was exactly how he felt about God just then—estranged and on speaking terms only from a distance. The Father in heaven seemed so far away.

Crisanto finally got up again. He just could not sleep. The crickets still chirped as he went to the front room and sat down to read his Bible. Lately, he had been having trouble connecting with his congregations spiritually. Maybe reading a few of God's promises would help.

He lit a lamp and, as he picked up his Bible, it fell open to the book of John. "Let not your heart be troubled; you believe in God, believe also in Me." His eyes quickly scanned the verses. "In My Father's house are many mansions; if it were not so, I would have told you. I go to prepare a place for you. And if I go and prepare a place for you, I will come again and receive you to Myself; that where I am, there you may be also" (John 14:1–3, NKJV).

That is a comforting passage, Crisanto thought. How timely to read something so relevant while he was discouraged and needed something to help him relax and go back to sleep.

And then his eyes dropped a few lines lower in the chapter. "If you love Me, keep My commandments" (verse 15, NKJV). *Hmm, that is an odd verse to be in the same chapter with verses one to three,* Crisanto thought. Hardly relevant to the problems he was facing in his own life and with his church congregations.

He closed the Bible, put it back on its little table and extinguished the lamp; then he again returned to his bed to lie down. "Lord, You know how hard it has been these many years since Imee died, and You know I want to serve You," Crisanto prayed. "Show me how I can do that better, Lord. Show me how to help my congregations as their pastor, and please show me how I can be happy."

He must have dropped off to sleep shortly after his prayer because suddenly the sun was streaming through his bedroom window. Strangely enough, he didn't remember anything from the night before.

Amihan was no longer in bed, and he could hear dishes clinking in the kitchen as she made breakfast.

When Crisanto had dressed and prepared for the day, he went out to join Amihan. They were just sitting down for a breakfast of eggs, fried rice, and *tocino* (carmelized pork) when he heard someone calling his name. "Señor Crisanto, please excuse me, sir, but I must speak with you this morning."

Crisanto went to the door. It was Dakila, one of his members from his congregation in Natonin. He could tell the man had something on his mind because he was holding his hat in his hands and turning it round and round nervously. Dakila did that a lot when he talked in public.

Crisanto leaned out through the open doorway. "I'm sitting down to eat breakfast with my wife. Would you join us, Dakila?"

"Si, señor, if it's no trouble."

"Come in, come in, then." Crisanto beckoned to his friend. "Get another plate, Amihan," he called. "We have a guest."

"What's on your mind?" Crisanto asked, as he passed Dakila a plate of rice and *tocino*.

"Well, sir, I've had the strangest dream. Twice now, actually, and it has been troubling me. After the first time, I just thought it strange; but when I dreamed it for the second time last night, I woke suddenly and couldn't sleep any longer."

Crisanto nodded. "I did not sleep well last night myself." He took another spoonful of rice. "I guess we are not so young anymore, my friend."

Dakila half-smiled and then hurried on. "No, I suppose not. Anyway, in my dream I was standing in our church and reading the Ten Commandments on the wall at the front. And as I looked, I saw a dove come down from heaven and alight on the fourth commandment, from which a glorious light was shining." Dakila had stopped eating and was looking at Crisanto earnestly. "So I was wondering, what do you think it means? It is a strange dream, don't you think?"

Crisanto nodded slowly. "I must agree with you, my friend. It is quite strange."

"But what does it mean, Pastor Crisanto?" Dakila's expression showed his concern. "Should I be worried about it?"

"*Hmm,* I cannot tell you if you should be worried, my friend, but this I can tell you. It is an important dream. That you dreamed of this twice would not be so important, maybe. We all dream things more than once from time to time. But this dream is about the Ten Commandments of God; and to me, that makes it more important."

"Can you explain it, Pastor?"

"Maybe I can, and maybe I cannot." Crisanto's brow knit in furrows. "But it seems to me that a dove is a very important symbol for Christians. Many times in the Bible, God used the coming of a dove to represent something special. The story of Noah's flood has a dove in it when the Flood was ending. And then, of course, when Jesus was baptized a dove came down and landed on Jesus' head, when the Father said Jesus was His beloved Son."

"So what does this mean for me? What can the bird on the Ten Commandments mean? And why was there a light on the fourth commandment?"

"The bird is a special sign, perhaps. But the fourth commandment? I wonder,"

Crisanto began, and then got a faraway look in his eyes.

"What is it, Pastor Crisanto? What are you thinking?" Dakila gripped Crisanto's arm.

Part 2: New Sabbath Congregation in Natonin

Well, this morning I could not sleep. I awoke and was remembering my little girl, Imee, and then I could not go back to sleep out of discouragement. So I got up and read some verses from the book of John to give me comfort. And one of the verses I read said that if we love God, we must obey His commandments. Here, let me read it to you."

Crisanto got his Bible and turned to the fourteenth chapter of John. "It says, 'If you love Me, keep My commandments.' Now that's a very simple verse," he added, "and I think it has a very simple message. Just the way God likes it. He doesn't usually send complicated messages. He sends ones that even children can understand."

Dakila's eyes got big. "So you think this message is really from God?"

"I think it must be." Crisanto grew serious. "It cannot be from Satan. The message is only good and points us to God's holy law. Satan would not do that."

"And the fourth commandment with the light on it?"

Crisanto frowned. "Yes, that commandment. I've always wondered about that fourth commandment, and—*hmm*, why don't we look at the commandments and see what they say? It may be that the Lord has light for us in that fourth commandment."

"But Pastor Crisanto, we have the Ten Commandments at the front of the church." Dakila sounded surprised. "You know them by heart and can say every one."

"Yes, you are right, but we must be missing something here, my friend. If God is trying to tell us something, we need to study it. He will show us what is truth. You can count on it. He never leaves His children in darkness for long.

"Let's look at the Ten Commandments for ourselves. They are in Exodus, chapter twenty," Crisanto said, as he turned the pages of his Bible, "and the verses on the fourth commandment are . . . verses eight to eleven. OK, let's read it together.

" 'Remember the Sabbath day, to keep it holy,' " Crisanto read aloud, knowing Dakila could not actually read. " 'Six days you shall labor and do all your work, but the seventh day is the Sabbath of the LORD your God. In it you shall do no work: you, nor your son, nor your daughter, nor your male servant, nor your female servant, nor your cattle, nor your stranger who is within your gates. For in six days the LORD made the heavens and the earth, the sea, and all that is in them, and rested the seventh day. Therefore the LORD blessed the Sabbath day and hallowed it' [NKJV].

"There you have it." Crisanto paused a moment longer looking at the verses. "God wants us to remember His Sabbath day because He blessed it and made it holy."

"Yes, but what does the part about the seventh day mean?" Dakila frowned as he listened to Crisanto's every word. "I know we should not work on Sunday because that is God's holy day, but why does it talk about the seventh day?"

"*Hmm,* good question." Crisanto's voice faded away as he read through the verses again silently. "This is very interesting," he added when he had finished. "It says God rested on the seventh day after He had made everything, and that's why He made the Sabbath sacred and holy."

"OK." Now it was Dakila's turn to think for a moment. "So, we worship as God has asked every Sunday. That makes sense, right?"

"No; actually, it doesn't make sense."

"Why not?" Dakila raised his eyebrows.

Crisanto got a very serious look on his face. "Because Sunday is not the seventh day of the week."

Dakila's jaw dropped a bit. "Oh Señor Crisanto! You are right. Sunday is not the seventh day. Saturday is."

"Exactly, and we have been keeping the wrong day holy."

"But how can this be? We keep the day all of the other Christians keep. Why would Christians be worshiping on the wrong day?"

"I don't know." Crisanto looked up from his Bible. "But we need to find out."

Crisanto studied his Bible all morning with Dakila and found more texts that confirmed that the seventh day is the Sabbath: Genesis 2:1–3; Ezekiel 11:20; Isaiah 66:23. He had always thought of himself as knowledgeable about the Scriptures, but now he realized he actually knew very little about the Sabbath.

By the end of the day, Crisanto was convinced this new insight about the Sabbath was from God. More important, he was convinced the seventh day was the Sabbath. Sunday was not God's holy day as he had been taught; Saturday was. According to the Bible, the Sabbath had always been God's sign between His people and Him. God's plan for the Sabbath had not changed down through the ages. It was still His chosen day, sanctified, and made holy for His people to enjoy.

Crisanto was a changed man because of this Sabbath discovery, and he began asking everyone he knew about where he could find other seventh-day keepers. "Are there Sabbath keepers in the villages of Mountain Province?" he wondered. "Do I need to travel to some distant city to find them?"

A new century had dawned, and the worldwide mission work of Seventh-day Adventists was growing. But Crisanto had no idea about the Seventh-day Adventist movement. He did not know there were other people in his country, and all over the world, who loved the truth about the Sabbath.

He had no idea whom he was looking for, but he decided to set out in search of them anyway. There had to people somewhere who believed in the holiness of

God's seventh-day Sabbath as he did—and he would find them.

He traveled eight days' journey south, asking people all along the way if they knew of anyone who was a seventh-day keeper. From Natonin through Bagabag and Bayombong and on down to San Jose City he searched, until he reached the outskirts of Manila, the capital of the Philippines. The going was slow, for there were no buses, trains, or planes in that part of the world at that time. Some days Crisanto caught a ride on an empty oxcart. Some days he rode boats across rivers, but most of the way he just walked.

At night, he slept where he could. Sometimes he stayed in the homes of relatives, sometimes under an awning at a market or in a storage shed on a farm. Most often he just stayed out in the open air, sleeping beside a little fire he had made to cook his meal. He was sure there were wild animals and bandits to fear, but he had no time to worry about such things. His heavenly Father would have to protect him from such dangers. His one goal now was to find the people of the seventh-day Sabbath.

"Yes, I've heard of such a people," an old man told him one day when he was passing through the marketplace in Bonifacio. "You can find the seventh-day keepers at the Seventh-day Adventist Mission in a town called Pasay."

The hour was late and there was no time to go on that night, but Crisanto was very excited now. He was so near his goal. Not surprisingly, he slept restlessly and was up again at the crack of dawn to make the final leg of his journey.

Later that day, he found the seventh-day keepers at the mission station in Pasay, just as the old man said he would, and he was jubilant. After coming all this way, through the hardships of travel, sleeping in uncomfortable conditions, and eating little or nothing at all some days, he had finally arrived. The Seventh-day Adventists were indeed the people of the seventh day, for they truly understood the biblical importance of the Sabbath. From the days of Creation to the days of Jesus and to the joyful celebration of the Sabbath in the earth made new, the special day had significance. And just as Crisanto had learned for himself from the Bible, the Sabbath was clearly God's sign for His last-day people.

But Crisanto was surprised to find the Seventh-day Adventists were also teaching other new things from the Bible as well. The truth about what happens when a person dies was startling, and so was the discovery that there is no eternally burning hell. He learned about salvation by grace and tithing, and that, according to the Bible, *tocino* was a forbidden food.

However, it was the promise about the soon coming of Jesus that surprised Crisanto the most. He now realized the Second Coming wasn't just an idea about life after death somewhere. It was the promise of the real return of Jesus to take His children home to heaven. According to the Bible, the coming of Jesus was going to happen soon—sometime in the near future. The prophecies in the Bible made that part very clear.

Crisanto stayed at the mission for more than a week. There was so much to learn; and at times, he was tempted to think that the new ideas he was hearing could not be true. But these truths were all in the Bible, as the Adventists so carefully showed him during their studies with him, and he finally decided that the biblical evidence was enough for him. He accepted the great truths he had learned from the Bible and was baptized by immersion.

Then taking with him many tracts and books to help him teach the good news to his church members, he headed back for Natonin.

Not everyone accepted the truths Pastor Crisanto brought home; but many did, and a new Adventist congregation was formed. It was a new day for them all, and everyone rejoiced when Crisanto became the pastor of this new church.

And the villagers rejoiced. God had sent a dove and the fourth commandment in the miracle of a dream to point the way to heaven. For them, eternal life was a reality now, and they knew their lives would never be the same.

Impossible Dream

Part 1: "I Dreamed I Saw Those Guys!"

Victor awoke with a start and lay on his back, staring up at the ceiling. He rubbed the sleep from his eyes and yawned. *Why did I dream such a thing?* In his dream, he saw two foreigners standing on the sidewalk on the main street of Santiago. They were reading aloud from a book, and it sounded like the Bible. He could still see their faces in his mind's eye. They looked to be nice young gentlemen, but he had no idea who they were or why he would dream such a thing.

He yawned again. *No matter. It was just a dream.* Dreams didn't mean anything, except as a way to clear the mind of nonsense and the troubles from the day before. At least, that was his theory.

He got out of bed and went to the basin of water sitting on his nightstand to wash his face. Then he ran his fingers through his hair, pulled on his trousers, suspenders, and shirt, and headed down the stairs. The smell of breakfast already filled the air, and he savored the delicious aromas of his mother's cooking. Fried potatoes, sausages, eggs, and crêpes were the usual. *Mmm!* What a meal!

Victor ate with gusto. He and his older brother Eduardo were the sons of Celine and Matthias Thomann, Swiss immigrants to the coast of Chile some twelve years before. Now they were cabinetmakers in Santiago and were known for their careful work.

"Will you be going out with that girl this evening, young man?" his mother asked as he sat down at the breakfast table.

"Yes, Mother," he answered respectfully, trying to stay busy eating his potatoes and eggs. On Friday evenings, Victor usually went out with his friends, and he did enjoy the company of a certain young girl in the community, not that he was serious about her.

"Well, mind that you don't forget to be home on time," she told him. "Your reputation is more important than that girl."

"Her name is Camila, Mother."

"All right, Camila it is, then. Be sure to have her home early, and be back here by ten o'clock."

"Yes, ma'am." Victor finished the food on his plate, sat back in his chair, and waited for his father to read the morning Bible chapter. This was the family habit—and a good one—though Victor didn't always appreciate it as much as he should have. After all, the chapters his father chose were rather long ones sometimes. Right now, they were stuck in Jeremiah, and Jeremiah could get pretty dry.

" 'For I know the plans I have for you,' declares the LORD, 'plans to prosper you and not to harm you, plans to give you hope and a future. Then you will call on me and come and pray to me, and I will listen to you. You will seek me and find me when you seek me with all your heart' " (Jeremiah 29:11–13, NIV).

Victor stared at his father. *Is that really a chapter from Jeremiah that Father is reading? Guess I was wrong about the prophet Jeremiah,* he thought to himself. *The man must have been a pretty good writer to say all that.*

After finishing the chapter, Matthias prayed, and then they went to their work assignments for the day. All that morning Victor and Eduardo worked in the family's cabinetmaking shop. The year had been good for their business. While many small businesses were still trying to pull themselves out of the slump of the early 1890s, 1895 had been kind to them. Matthias's work ethic—work hard, be honest, and treat the customer like a king—was paying off. *Those are good words of advice,* Victor thought, but he was sure that God was blessing their business too.

Late that afternoon Victor and his brother prepared for the party his mother had teased him about. Both boys got their hair cut, took their weekly baths, and then dressed in their starched white shirts, black ties, and waistcoats.

"How can you stand that Camila?" Eduardo rolled his eyes. "She is the silliest thing I've ever seen."

"Yeah, but she's beautiful." Victor grinned as he tried tying the knot in his tie for the fourth time. "You're just jealous."

"Jealous? Why would I be jealous?"

"Because you don't have a girl," Victor reminded his brother.

"Hey," Eduardo grinned at his brother, "I've got lots of time to find a girl, but let me make something very clear. When I court a girl, it won't be someone like Camila, who happens to come from the most superstitious family in town."

Victor stopped arguing at that comment. He couldn't deny his brother's accusation. Eduardo was right; Camila and her family were superstitious. Terribly so, which was quite common for Chilean Catholic families. They were afraid of black cats and black butterflies, and pretty much anything black, including black at a funeral. On the one hand, if a family member dreamed about a funeral, it meant someone was going to get married soon. On the other hand, if one dreamed about a wedding, it meant someone was going to die. If the moon was dark, that was bad luck; but if you had money in your pockets when the moon was full, it meant you would prosper during the coming month.

The two brothers went to the party early that evening. It was a traditional festive Chilean party for one of the girls who was turning fifteen; but Victor didn't enjoy himself as much as he thought he would because the party wasn't well planned. Some of his friends just sat around and talked, and some played silly games, but others drank quite a bit. Victor hadn't been raised to behave like that, and it made him feel a bit strange to be around people who acted so foolishly.

On the way home, he kept thinking about his brother's comments about Camila. "Maybe Eduardo is right. What is the point of spending time with Camila and her friends?" he asked himself. "They are so different from my own family—so shallow and silly and yet very superstitious about many things."

Maybe it's time I started getting a little more serious about life, he thought. *Maybe it's time I started acting in ways that will make my parents proud of me. Maybe God needs more of a place in my life.*

The next morning was Saturday; when Victor awakened, his dream about the two men on the street corner the morning before suddenly came to mind. A strange sensation came over him as he realized that he still held the picture of the two young men clearly in his mind. *Why am I remembering this dream so vividly? Who are these two men? Is there something important I should know about them?* He hadn't shared the dream with anyone because he hadn't thought it mattered. Maybe he was wrong about that.

He lay in bed for several more minutes, thinking about the dream as he stared up at the ceiling, and then closed his eyes again. "Dear God," he prayed, "why did I dream such a thing? Is it important for me? Is it some kind of a sign from You? I have a strange feeling You're trying to tell me something."

He got out of his bed, knelt beside it, and continued praying. "I want to give You my life, Lord. If You've got something You want me to do for You, please show me. I want to make something of myself. Help me, Lord, to find Your plan for my life."

He got up and prepared for the day, dressing in a hurry and getting down to breakfast in record time. As usual, the morning meal was wonderful, and then the family had their Bible devotion again. " 'You will be my people, and I will be your God' " (Jeremiah 30:22, NIV). Matthias was reading the next chapter in Jeremiah, and Victor listened more attentively, taking the verses to heart.

If this is what it means to give your life to God, then I want it, Victor thought. *Just think of it! I will be one of His chosen people, and He will be my God.* It sounded really good, knowing that he would be safe eternally if he put his trust in God.

On Saturdays Matthias didn't ask his sons to help in the cabinet shop. It was their day off to do what they wanted with their time. After a leisurely breakfast, Victor and Eduardo went down to the race track to watch some horse races; afterward they bought lunch in a little outdoor café. In the afternoon, they went for a stroll down the main avenue in town. This was the busiest thoroughfare in

Santiago, and there always was plenty to see and do.

Heavily loaded wagons lumbered down the cobblestones of the main street, and buggies sped past in a hurry. Children ran, playing in the street, dodging the pedestrians and men on horseback.

Shops were at their busiest on Saturday. Watchmakers, jewelers, and tailors all competed for the window shoppers of Santiago. Restaurants and hotels were found on every street corner, and behind them in the alleys were the blacksmith shops and wheelwrights and stables.

On the sidewalks, vendors were hawking their hot oven-baked *empanadas* made with diced meat, onions, and olives. An organ-grinder with a little monkey on his shoulder played music for people as they passed. Newspaper boys were selling newspapers, and two young men were reading out loud from a Bible.

> "Bless the LORD, O my soul;
> And all that is within me, bless His holy name!
> Bless the LORD, O my soul,
> And forget not all His benefits:
> Who forgives all your iniquities,
> Who heals all your diseases" (Psalm 103:1–3, NKJV).

One of the young men was speaking in a heavily accented Spanish that clearly suggested he was still trying to learn the language.

> "As the heavens are high above the earth,
> So great is His mercy toward those who fear Him;
> As far as the east is from the west,
> So far has He removed our transgressions from us" (verses 11, 12, NKJV).

Suddenly, Victor grabbed his brother by the arm. "Hey! Those are the two guys I dreamed about," he said excitedly.

"You what?" Eduardo stared at his brother.

"I dreamed I saw those guys," Victor repeated. "It was those same guys. Night before last, I dreamed I saw them standing right here on this very street corner reading from a book. In my dream, they were doing just like they're doing right now—reading from the Bible."

Part 2: "You Must Be Messengers From God"

Those guys?" Eduardo glanced at the two strangers, and then at Victor. "You know those guys? How's that possible?"

"I don't know. I have no idea; but I'm telling you, I dreamed it!"

Eduardo squinted at his brother. "Well, you must have seen them somewhere, or you wouldn't have dreamed about them. Maybe you've seen them here in town but just don't remember."

"No, I don't think so. And besides, that's not the point! It's not about whether I've seen them before. It's that I saw those two guys in my dream, standing right here on this sidewalk just like they are right now, reading from the Bible. I'm telling you, these are the guys." Victor looked dazed. "This is really weird."

And then Victor remembered the prayer he had prayed in bed earlier that day. Hadn't he thought the dream might be a sign from God? Hadn't he knelt by his bed and asked God to reveal Himself and a plan for his life? Well maybe this was it. Perhaps the dream was coming true!

Victor walked right up to the two young men. "Hi, my name is Victor Thomann," he said. "I've seen you two guys before. You must be messengers from God."

"Messengers from God?" one of the young men replied. "Well now, that's exactly what we are—missionary messengers from God. My name is Fred Bishop." He held out his hand. "And this is Thomas Davis. We just got into town. Where did you say you've seen us before?"

Victor started to explain, but then saw the look on his brother's face. "I'll tell you what," he continued. "You come home with us for supper, and I'll tell you all about it. You guys look like you could use a good meal." He grinned. "You won't regret it, I promise! Believe me, my mother can really cook."

And so Fred and Thomas went home with the brothers for supper, and what a good time they had! Victor told them all about his dream, how he had seen Fred and Thomas standing on the street corner, reading from their Bibles.

"In my dream, I remember hearing Fred trying to read in Spanish. It was amazing because I heard him reading the exact same verses they were reading this afternoon when we found them. 'Bless the LORD, O my soul,' Fred was saying over and over. That's why it stuck in my head. And he was talking about the east and west in that chapter too."

Everyone was surprised to hear about the dream—most of all Eduardo. "Why didn't you tell me about this before?" he asked.

Victor shrugged. "I don't know. It only happened the night before last. I guess I thought it wasn't really that important. I mean, I never actually thought it would come true! And besides, I was sure you would laugh at me. Really now, be honest, if I had told you I thought the dream was going to come true, would you have believed me? How often does someone tell you what he or she dreamed, and then the dream comes true?"

"You've got a point," Eduardo admitted.

Then they all sat down to eat, and what a meal it was! The brothers were right; Celine could cook like nobody else Fred and Thomas had ever known. She made potatoes with dark gravy, hot buttered corn, and biscuits that were light and fluffy. She also served several traditional Chilean dishes that were favorites in the area. *Empanadas,* and *pastel de choclo* made with ground corn and meat, and a savory soup called *carbonada.*

And when she brought out her famous pork roast, the men of the family all groaned with delight. She carved it and then began serving it on everyone's plates. However, when she came to Fred and Thomas, they politely declined.

"You don't like my pork roast?" she asked. "The gravy is rich and spicy. It's Victor's and Eduardo's favorite."

"Oh, I'm sure it's the best around." Fred glanced at Thomas. "We used to eat pork but not anymore."

"Why not?"

"Well, the Bible tells us we shouldn't."

"It does?" Celine put the plate of roast down, clearly interested now in this conversation.

Fred explained, "According to the book of Leviticus, some meats aren't good for the body, and pork is one of them."

"Really, now. Well, I've never heard of such a thing," she said. "Tell us more."

And so Fred and Thomas gave the family a Bible study on the kinds of foods that are harmful to put into the human body. Everyone was intrigued with the topic as they continued to eat the good things on the table; when they were finished, they all moved into the parlor to hear more.

"Tell us how you got here, and where you've been in Chile," Victor said. "We've been here for more than twelve years, but I bet you've already been more places than we have."

"Well, let's see, we first came to Chile over a year ago," Thomas began. "We landed in the port in Valparaiso with several suitcases of books but very little money. In fact, after paying the man who rowed us ashore, we had only one *peso* between us. Fred immediately tried selling a book called *Bible Readings,* but neither of us knew any Spanish, so we had no luck.

"Then a sailor pointed us to a part of town where English settlers lived, and before that day was done, Fred had sold six of the books. Now we had money enough for a while so we could eat, at least.

"Things did get better, and we decided to travel north, where we sold books in towns such as Rosita, Huara, and San Donato. We had a lot of books with us printed in Spanish, and the one that sold the best was *Patriarchs and Prophets* by Ellen G. White.

"As the weeks went by, we worked our way back down the coast, selling in small towns mostly. We always prayed that God would prepare the way before us, and He has never failed us."

"And Santiago? We've never been in a town quite like Santiago," Fred added. "Your town is full of churches, but it's also full of superstition. We're not sure which of the two has more influence here: the church or superstition."

"You can say that again." Victor rolled his eyes. "We can't imagine why superstition has taken such a strong hold on these people!"

"Well, you can be sure Satan is the one behind all of the superstitious beliefs," Thomas replied. "Superstition is based on fear, and Satan is the father of fear."

"I hope we're not offending you," Fred apologized. "You folks have been so good to us already, but to be completely honest, we aren't liked very much by some Catholics. I can assure you we've had a lot of scary experiences, and some downright dangerous ones where priests wanted us dead. I guess they don't appreciate us teaching the people what the Bible says about things like graven images to the saints and life after death."

"And what does the Bible say about life after death?" Victor asked with growing interest. These two visitors from America were the most exciting travelers to come through Santiago in a long time. They were intelligent, and it was clear they were truly men of God, missionary messengers sent from the Lord, as Fred had put it.

The next evening Victor and Eduardo invited friends over to hear the stories Fred and Thomas were telling and how they had become acquainted with Victor and his family. It was an exciting time for them all as they realized that God had performed a miracle for them to get the group together.

Fred conducted a Bible study for everyone that evening. He would read a verse for them in his English Bible, and then they would all read the verse from their Spanish Bibles. They were so engrossed in a fascinating study of what happens after death that they failed to notice the time until the clock on the mantel struck midnight. They were so eager to listen to the two missionaries who had been sent by God to bring them the words of life that no one had noticed the time.

The following evening, they got together again—and the next. By now, they were studying the Ten Commandments and beginning to understand the reality of what it means to truly worship God. "We cannot expect God's blessings when we make images to the saints," Thomas said. "He has forbidden us to do that. Images lower our understanding of God's greatness. Are we not, indeed, attempting to make gods out of these men and women who have died and await our Savior's return? They are not in heaven. They are dead and have no power to hear us or answer our prayers at all. Only God can answer our prayers."

Other discussions on the commandments led them to a study of the true seventh-day Sabbath; and by the next weekend, they all met at Victor's house to keep the Sabbath. What a testimony to the power of God in the life of a young man like Victor, who was willing to listen to the voice of God! Truly, the angels of heaven sang praises to God for Victor's part in the conversion of many in Santiago, and the missionary spirit that brought the three angels' messages to the city of Santiago.

Fred Bishop and Thomas Davis eventually left Chile to serve God elsewhere, but Victor continued to work for the Lord. He helped raise a substantial con-gregation in Santiago and became one of its first pastors. Then he and Eduardo began publishing Adventist literature and became the first editors of the Spanish *Signs of the Times*® in Chile. Victor grew into a great leader for the church work in Chile, and Eduardo became an evangelist and editor of the Seventh-day Adventist publishing house in Chile. Together they traveled far and wide to proclaim the message they had come to love.

And all because of a dream. God saw fit to reveal Himself in a most remarkable revelation that sparked the interest of those who were searching for truth. When Jesus returns again someday soon, He will find many who learned about the three angels' messages during the hundred years since Victor Thomann took that first step to welcome complete strangers whom he had seen in a dream.

Miracle Catch

Part 1: American Missionary Arrives in Pakhoi

On the Gulf of Tonkin there once lived a poor fisherman named Quingshan. Like countless generations of his ancestors before him, he made his living fishing from a little skiff in the seaside town of Pakhoi. His father had fished this stretch of water before him, as had his grandfather, and his grandfather's grandfather.

Every day at sunset, he and his sixteen-year-old son, Liang, pushed off from the docks to spend their night fishing on the ocean. After hoisting the sail, they always arrived quickly at the inlet of the bay, where the incoming tide made the fishing better. They would drop their nets in an arching circle behind the boat and then settle down to wait. Sometimes they had to wait only an hour or two for the shoals of fish to swim into their nets; but other times, they had to wait much of the night. Sometimes they caught scores of fish, and then other times they caught almost nothing.

It was a simple but hard life as Quingshan tried to catch enough fish to support the family. But it was all he knew. There were those in the community who raised a little rice, and some who made their living as vendors in the local markets; but fishing was the mainstay of the economy in the little town of Pakhoi. As the fishing went, so went the prosperity of the community.

One day, quite unexpectedly, an American missionary arrived in town. His name was Pastor Edwin Wilbur, and he promised that he had a story to tell.

"I've come to share the good news of the three angels' messages," he told the town elders.

"Who are these three angels?" the elders asked in surprise. "Why have we not heard about them before? Li Meng, our medicine man, has said nothing about this to us. He isn't in town now; but when he returns, we will ask him right away."

"The three angels have been sent by God at this time in earth's history to warn us about the end of the world," Pastor Wilbur replied.

The elders looked at each other in alarm. "Then this is very important, and we must not delay. Please, stay in our town and tell us about these angels and their messages. Where are you staying?"

"I have no permanent place to stay yet," Pastor Wilbur replied. "Right now I am staying in a little tent I have set up near the beach."

"Then we will build you a house," the elders promised. "You must feel welcome among us with such an important message from God."

And so they began the task of building a little house out of bamboo and palm-frond thatch on the edge of town. Everybody helped, even Quingshan and his son, though they had to go without sleep to do it. Wooden poles were brought from the forest and set in the ground, and bamboo was used to make the framework of the roof. Palm leaves were woven together to make a watertight roof, and bamboo poles were split for the flooring.

The little house was up in under a week, and what a nice little dwelling it was for the missionary and his family.

"Thank you so much for building me a house," Pastor Wilbur said. "Now where will we have the meetings? Do you have a building big enough for all the people who may want to come and hear about the three angels?"

The elders looked at one another in dismay. "We do not," they said with disappointment in their voices, "but we will." Immediately, they set about instructing the townsfolk to build a meeting house. And so a second building went up next to the first one, but this one was much larger.

Within three weeks, both buildings were finished, and the elders smiled with satisfaction. "Now we can hear about your messages from the angels, and we have a nice meeting house so everyone can come. Are you ready to speak tonight?" the elders asked in earnest.

Pastor Wilbur smiled. "I am always ready to speak about the three angels."

And so it was that scores showed up that first evening, and Quingshan was one of the first to arrive. "We'll just have to push off from the beach a bit later than usual," he told his son, Liang. "I don't want to completely lose out on the fishing tonight, but I don't want to miss the meetings either."

Everyone crowded into the meeting house and sat on the floor, but there was not enough space. Big as the building was, it still was not big enough to hold all the people who wanted to hear Pastor Wilbur speak. Some crowded around the doorway, and others had to peer through the little holes and slits in the walls made of palm fronds. Some of the younger ones managed to climb trees outside and watch through the open windows.

Quingshan and his family enjoyed that first evening very much, as did all of the folks who had attended. It was a perfect night for such a meeting. Pastor Wilbur set up a picture roll of Bible pictures at the front. Lit torches were placed around the room, but care was taken to keep them away from the walls and the roof of the meeting house. The last thing they needed was to have their meeting house burn down after all the hard work they had put into building it.

That first night Pastor Wilbur told the story of the three angels in the Bible, where they were from, and why they were being sent from God.

"God has given the three angels' messages for us, and they can be found in this little black Book." Pastor Wilbur held up his Bible. "Tonight, I will read the messages to you, but there is not enough time to explain them well, so I will have to continue on with that part tomorrow evening.

"Now here is what the message says, 'I saw another angel flying in the midst of heaven, having the everlasting gospel to preach to those who dwell on the earth—to every nation, tribe, tongue, and people—saying with a loud voice, "Fear God and give glory to Him, for the hour of His judgment has come; and worship Him who made heaven and earth, the sea and springs of water."

" 'And another angel followed, saying, "Babylon is fallen, is fallen, that great city, because she has made all nations drink of the wine of the wrath of her fornication."

" 'Then a third angel followed them, saying with a loud voice, "If anyone worships the beast and his image, and receives his mark on his forehead or on his hand, he himself shall also drink of the wine of the wrath of God, which is poured out full strength into the cup of His indignation. He shall be tormented with fire and brimstone in the presence of the holy angels and in the presence of the Lamb. And the smoke of their torment ascends forever and ever; and they have no rest day or night, who worship the beast and his image, and whoever receives the mark of his name." . . . Here is the patience of the saints; here are those who keep the commandments of God and the faith of Jesus' [Revelation 14:6, 7, 12, NKJV]. We find those messages in a section of the book called Revelation that God included in His Holy Word, the Bible," Pastor Wilbur said.

The oldest elder at the meeting stood to speak. "These are very important messages," he said solemnly. "No other missionary has told us these things. We need to hear more. We must know what God wants us to do to escape the coming danger."

Quingshan nodded his head in agreement. He couldn't have said it better himself. He was very impressed—and a little afraid at the thought of a coming judgment from God. He wanted to hear more, but realized it was growing late. He needed to get out on the ocean for the night's fishing.

Fortunately, Pastor Wilbur was finishing his talk for the evening. "We don't have more time this evening," the pastor told everyone. "However, if you come again tomorrow evening, we'll continue."

And with that Quingshan was off to the beach, where his boat was ready to sail. Before the evening meeting had begun, he and Liang had prepared the nets and put food in the boat for the long night of fishing.

Part 2: The First Sabbath Keepers

Quingshan and his son pushed off from the beach and set sail for the entrance to the bay, knowing that most of the good spots had already been taken by other fishermen. That was the price he was paying for starting late, but he didn't care. He had heard words of truth at the evening meeting, probably the most important ones in all of his life. And if everything Pastor Wilbur had to say was as interesting as his first message, then Quingshan knew he did not want to miss even one meeting.

This evening Quingshan was hoping for a good catch as usual, even if they had gotten a late start. The evening was pleasant, and the moon was already well up above the eastern horizon. Its pale blue disk was ghostlike, giving almost no light. When fishing, the less light the better, because fish generally do not like to come to the surface when there is bright moonlight.

Quingshan loved these nights out on the ocean. As he looked up at the night sky, he was thinking there had never been a more peaceful place on earth. Myriads of stars were splashed across the heavens. In the sky above, he could hear the call of birds swooping back and forth in search of insects on the wing. Now and then, he heard a splash as a fish jumped clear of the water.

They were far from the shore now. Behind him, Quingshan could see the faint twinkling of lights from Pakhoi. Ahead he could see dozens of fishing boats huddled together in the dim moonlight. Liang pulled down the sail, Quingshan threw out the nets, and then they both settled down for a long night of waiting for the fish to "run." If they were patient and lucky, maybe they would get a good catch.

And fortunately, they did have a good catch that night. It came not long before dawn. "Aren't we lucky?" Quingshan exclaimed to his son, as they sailed back to shore near dawn. "We got out on the bay late because we were at the meeting, and we still got a good catch."

Liang was silent for a few moments and then quietly said, "Maybe that is God's way of rewarding us for wanting to know about the three angels."

"Maybe," Quingshan replied, and to be honest, he had never thought such a thing was possible. *Can God do that for me?* he wondered. *Or more important, would God do that for me?*

The next evening, Quingshan and his son attended the meeting again before going out to fish. Again everyone listened attentively as Pastor Wilbur explained all about the three angels' messages and why God had sent them.

Each evening thereafter, Pastor Wilbur spoke to the people in the meeting house. Soon a group of serious worshipers had formed, and Quingshan and his son were among them. One Friday evening after the meeting, Pastor Wilbur surprised them all with an announcement.

"We would like to invite you all to come tomorrow morning for another meeting," he said. "Saturday is God's holy day, and it's the time my family and I worship the God of heaven."

The elders looked confused. "Saturday?" they asked. "Why not Sunday like all of the other missionaries who have come to the Gulf of Tonkin?"

"Because Saturday is the day on which God rested from His creation of the world," Pastor Wilbur explained. "He made the world in six days and then rested on the seventh. To celebrate how pleased He was with the beautiful things He had made, He blessed the seventh day and made it holy. We call it the Sabbath and worship Him on that day as He has commanded us in the Bible."

The elders bowed respectfully. "Then we must worship Him on the seventh day too. We will come again tomorrow morning."

The next morning the elders all showed up. The group of worshipers was smaller than in the evenings, but that was expected. Those who were vendors had to go to market; Saturday was a busy day for them. And the fishermen who had come home from fishing all night on the sea were at home sleeping. But Quingshan was there with his wife, Jiao, and his son. Quingshan and Liang were very tired, but they wanted to hear everything Pastor Wilbur had to say about the Sabbath.

That morning the worship service proved to be the turning point in Quingshan's life. He was astonished at how appealing the message of the Sabbath was! This business of having one day off in seven was a totally new idea for him, but it made good sense. Working all the time was not good for anyone, and he often felt worn out, fishing night after night after night.

But there was another thing he didn't quite understand about Sabbath observance. He did not fish during the day, so how would he keep Sabbath? Was God talking about daylight hours when He asked His people to keep the Sabbath day holy?

Pastor Wilbur nodded and smiled. "Good question, Quingshan. Actually, the time for worshiping God on His holy day is referring to the entire twenty-four-hour period on which the Sabbath falls. According to the Bible, that would be from sunset Friday to sunset Saturday."

From sunset Friday to sunset Saturday? Quingshan thought about that for a moment. If he followed God's instruction, he would have to skip work on Friday nights in order to honor the Sabbath. He would have to stay at home on Friday nights while all of the other fishermen went out as usual. That was a lot to consider. Could he make enough money to support his family if he didn't fish one night of every week? It was his livelihood. He would have to catch enough extra fish the other six nights to make up for what he would miss on Friday nights.

"It's a test from God," Pastor Wilbur told Quingshan. "No doubt about it, but God has promised us great blessings if we honor Him and His Sabbath. Isaiah says,

'If you turn away your foot from the Sabbath,
From doing your pleasure on My holy day,
And call the Sabbath a delight,

The holy day of the Lord honorable,
And shall honor Him, not doing your own ways,
Nor finding your own pleasure,
Nor speaking your own words,
Then you shall delight yourself in the Lord;
And I will cause you to ride on the high hills of the earth,
And feed you with the heritage of Jacob your father.
For the mouth of the Lord has spoken' [Isaiah 58:13, 14, NKJV]."

Quingshan thought about that for several days. He was a good man, a man of principle, accustomed to doing the right thing when he was sure it was the proper thing to do. Finally, after much prayer, he announced to his family, "Liang and I will not be fishing on Friday nights anymore. The Sabbath is God's holy day, and we will obey His instructions not to work on that day. We will not do our own business on the day that God has asked us to honor in remembrance of His creation."

His wife, Jiao, thought that Quingshan was being unrealistic. She had attended the Sabbath day service with him and had heard the same message he had heard, but she was not as convinced about it as he was. "You cannot support your family if you intend to skip one workday in seven," she scolded him. "No man can truly say he is a good provider if he refuses to work—and least of all men who are mere fishermen!"

Those words stung as Jiao reminded Quingshan of his humble station in life. That much he could not deny, but neither could he deny the feelings that had come over him as he heard the Words of Scripture about God's holy Sabbath day. He could see his wife's point of view, but the Holy Spirit had impressed him that the missionary was teaching the truth.

"We will keep the Sabbath," he said firmly. "We must do as God asks. We cannot disobey Him." Jiao wasn't happy, but Quingshan was the person who earned the family income, so she said nothing more.

In the weeks that followed, Pastor Wilbur covered many other topics from the Bible, and Quingshan embraced them all without reservation. Here was a religion that gave him hope for the future, unlike the Buddhist religion of his people.

Week by week, he and Liang never missed a meeting. And week by week, they honored the Sabbath by letting their fishing nets and boat rest on the shore from sundown Friday to sundown Saturday. Slowly, Quingshan began to see that God was indeed blessing them. He was rewarding them for coming to the meetings and obeying the command of the Lord that said, "Six days you shall labor and do all your work, but the seventh day is the Sabbath of the LORD your God" (Exodus 20:9, NKJV).

But Satan was not happy to see the gospel breaking new ground, and he certainly wasn't happy to see Quingshan and his family give their lives to God as Seventh-day Adventist Christians. So he set out to oppress the fisherman.

One evening at sunset, Quingshan and Liang pushed off from the beach a bit later than usual and found that all the good spots in the bay had been taken.

"Where did all the fishing boats come from?" Quingshan asked his son. "It seems there are many more boats now than there used to be."

And so they had to move their boat outside the shelter of the bay, into the open ocean. Quingshan dropped anchor and turned the boat into the oncoming waves, as Liang let down the nets. Gentle breezes were blowing in from the south, and the tidal currents were weaker than usual.

Father and son lay back against the gunwales of the shallow skiff to enjoy the sounds of the sea. Little was going on out on the ocean this time of evening, with the seagulls on shore for the night. The incoming tide slapped the sides of the boat, and the wind whispered through the simple riggings of the mast above. And always Quingshan could hear the rising and falling of the waves in the cross-currents of the ocean.

Part 3: A Storm Like a Monster

They waited for the familiar tug on the lines, but it never came. And then somewhere about the middle of the night Quingshan noticed a stiff breeze picking up. A breeze like that might mean nothing at all, but it could also mean trouble was on the way.

"Do you think there will be a storm?" Liang asked.

"Maybe," Quingshan took a handful of sticky rice from a pot in the bottom of the boat and began to put bits of it into his mouth. He held the pot of rice up to Liang and checked the night sky.

When a sudden gust of wind hit the side of the boat, making it dip in the waves, Quingshan stood to his feet. "I think we'd better return to port where we can anchor properly," he said with a sense of urgency in his voice. "Help me get the nets pulled in, Liang."

By now the fishermen in the other boats were working to get their nets in too. They called out to each other, shouting advice about the coming storm and the need to hurry. Most of the boats in the area had their sails up by now; but even as the wind hit the squares of heavy fabric, Quingshan could see the tall masts of the boats beginning to tip in the rising wind. He glanced up at the starry skies fast disappearing behind a covering of clouds and realized that getting into the bay where the waves were calmer wasn't going to be easy.

Zigzag patterns of lightning suddenly jumped from the sky, some of them dangerously close. The lightning sparked in fantastic tints of pink and yellow, and then almost bluish white. Sometimes the streaks of light struck quickly, and other times they arched slowly from the east almost to the west, as if trying to span the entire heavens.

And claps of thunder always followed. At the blaze of each lightning bolt,

Quingshan knew horrendous booms would follow. Sometimes one second after, sometimes two or three, when the bolts of lightning were farther away. The gigantic peals of rumbling thunder now seemed to split the sky in two, vibrating the boat, and fairly setting Quingshan's teeth on edge.

He was really worried now. They were so far from shore, and he knew it was going to take superhuman effort to get them safely back. But he had to do it for his son's sake!

"Tell me what to do!" Liang shouted as Quingshan grabbed a corner of the sail that had come loose and was whipping about wildly.

"You'd better hang on to that rudder, son," Quingshan shouted above the peals of thunder.

Liang jumped to the back of the boat and grabbed the long wooden handle. Quingshan hung on to the snapping sail with one hand and the side of the boat with the other. Waves churned this way and that, driving hard against the boat and sending up plumes of spray. Now and then, a wave higher than the rest would hit Quingshan's boat broadside, washing over the gunwales, and threatening to sink them.

He and his son both knew how to swim. That was not the problem. They had swum many times in the ocean and could last many hours even out on the open sea. But a storm like this was different. In wild, raging waters like this, it would probably be hard for a swimmer to last more than a few minutes!

Quingshan began to panic. He had thought they would have time to bring their boat to shore, but he had been mistaken. Now what could he do? The thought of their boat sinking filled his heart with terror. What if Liang drowned? What would he tell Jiao if he came back home without him? He would rather die himself than let Liang drown.

He was an experienced fisherman. But tonight things were different. The storm was doing strange things Quingshan had never seen a storm do before! The lightning and thunder were scary beyond words; the wind and waves were stronger and wilder than he would have thought possible. It was as if the storm was some giant monster trying to devour everything in its path. Even worse, it seemed the devil and his demons were in the storm, determined to sink every fishing boat on the ocean!

Flashes of lightning revealed fishing vessels in every direction pitching on the foaming ocean. Men shouted wildly as they bailed out their boats. Sails were torn from their masts and rudders from their moorings. Above the shrieking wind and the crashing of thunder, Quingshan could hear other fishermen screaming curses at the forces of evil and pleading with Buddha for help.

And then suddenly Quingshan thought of God. Where was He? Did He care that Quingshan and his son would lose everything if this storm didn't end soon? Did He understand that the two of them might drown out here on the mighty ocean? And what about the lives of all the other men in the fishing boats out on the sea? Their lives were at stake here too! Did they matter to God?

"Help us, Lord God of heaven!" Quingshan finally shouted above the raging storm. "Help us, or we'll die!"

A huge wave suddenly slammed against the side of Quingshan's boat, filling it dangerously. Liang was washed overboard, shouting as he went, but there seemed nothing Quingshan could do. "Please, God," he heard himself screaming, "save my son!" How he managed to throw a rope to Liang and pull him back to the boat wasn't clear to him.

And now they had to really bail fast because they were sinking from water inside the boat. The weather worsened when it began to rain. Sheets of rain descended upon them, driven by the howling wind, until Quingshan could see no farther than a few yards ahead.

They drifted on with the tide, bailing water, trying to keep themselves afloat, until Liang suddenly shouted, "I see a light! I see more lights!"

Sure enough, there were lights, many of them, and he knew now they were nearing the beach. "Thank You, Lord," was all he could say. He had no energy for anything else.

The rain was still pouring down, but the waves had grown smaller this close to the shore. They were able to make real progress. When the water was shallow enough, they hopped out into the water and dragged the boat up on the beach. Then they tied the boat with strong ropes to palm trees.

Part 4: Hunger, Illness, and Debt

As the rain stopped, Quingshan and the other fishermen had time to take stock of the damage done to their boats. Most of the sails had been torn loose, and many boats had lost them completely. Some of the masts had even been broken. Fishing gear was missing and nets shredded. Two boats had sunk in the bay.

Quingshan was thankful to God that he and Liang were alive; but when he examined his boat the next morning in daylight, he could see it was going to take days to repair—and lots of money. And he would have to buy some new nets.

He got a neighbor to help him repair his boat because he didn't know how to fix everything on the damaged skiff. The wooden boards on the hull had come loose and big cracks were now opening up. The boat was so badly damaged that Quingshan had no idea how they had even made it to shore.

"We should have drowned," Quingshan told Pastor Wilbur one day when he showed him the repairs they were making.

"But you didn't, and for one simple reason," the missionary pastor replied. "God has a work for you to do here in Pakhoi and on the Gulf of Tonkin. It's clear that He needs you."

Quingshan was greatly encouraged by Pastor Wilbur's words and stored them away in his heart. Surely God had a purpose for his life as the pastor had said! However, Quingshan's troubles were not over. One thing led to another in the costs of boat repairs and the gear that needed to be replaced. Before long, he had used up all of the money he kept hidden inside a can on a shelf in their kitchen.

What else could he do? He had to repair his boat and buy the fishing supplies the storm had taken. How else could he get out on the ocean again and provide for his family?

And then the catch each night began to diminish. No one knew why, but up and down all of the coast of China, fishermen reported the same thing. It was as if there were no more fish in the sea.

"What we've got is a famine of fish," Liang told Quingshan one morning when they came back again without a single fish. It was frightening to see how bad things had gotten. "Before, we used to complain if the fish we caught were small," Liang admitted. "Now we'd be glad to catch anything at all."

"The Lord will provide," Pastor Wilbur kept saying, and Quingshan was sure he was right. The question in his mind was, *When?*

And then an even worse tragedy struck. Quingshan's wife became sick, and he had to call for a doctor. After the doctor visited Jiao, he diagnosed her as having a sickness of the blood. This didn't surprise Quingshan.

"We've been so short on food for the last few months, how could we expect her to stay well?" Quingshan was distraught. Here he was trying to be a Seventh-day Adventist Christian by honoring God's holy Sabbath each week and faithfully attending church, but now he was a poorer man than he had been when he first became a Christian.

"I think God has forgotten us," he told Pastor Wilbur one Sabbath. "Why else would all of these things be happening to us?"

"All of these things are happening to you to test your faith in God," Pastor Wilbur assured him. "It won't last forever; I can promise you that. Think of it. Honestly, Quingshan, if God always gave us everything we wanted or needed, we wouldn't serve Him because we love Him. We would serve Him for all of the things we could get from Him. There are plenty of stories in the Bible that will support my point. The story of Job is one, and the one about Joseph in Egypt is another."

Pastor Wilbur took time the next Sabbath to read both stories to Quingshan, and the fisherman was inspired by the faithfulness of these two men during such hard times. "I want to be like them," Quingshan quietly told the missionary.

"That's good," Pastor Wilbur added. "I'm proud of you. Like Job and Joseph, you can be faithful to God no matter what happens. Remember, in the end, God blessed Job and Joseph, giving them everything they had lost—and more besides. God is never unwilling to help His children in their times of need, Quingshan. He just makes us wait sometimes to help us grow in faith.

"And let me tell you something else," Pastor Wilbur added, opening his Bible.

"The real problem here is not God. It is Satan. Paul says that 'we wrestle not against flesh and blood, but against principalities, against powers, against the rulers of the darkness of this world, against spiritual wickedness in high places' [Ephesians 6:12, KJV].

"So, you see, Satan is very angry right now because you and your son have given your lives to serve God. He is trying to discourage you, but God won't let him continue his harassment forever."

Again Quingshan was impressed with Pastor Wilbur's faith, and he was hopeful that the missionary's words would indeed come true.

Unfortunately, things still did not get any better right away. Quingshan had to borrow a little more for more boat repairs and a little more for his wife's medicine. Within a few months, he was living the nightmare he feared most: he was in debt.

It wasn't a huge sum as debts go, but it seemed to be an astronomical amount for a poor fisherman. This discouraged him, and he knew he and Liang would have to work all the harder to escape the noose that circumstances had made.

Quingshan prayed much about his problems, but it seemed his prayers went no higher than the ceiling. He went to church every Sabbath, but he was no longer focusing on the blessings he was receiving from being in God's house. More and more, he was worrying; and less and less, he was praising God for the gifts of family, forgiveness, and the hope of salvation.

Pastor Wilbur prayed often with Quingshan and asked that God would lift the spiritual shadows of doubt and darkness; but as the weeks passed, Quingshan's discouragement grew.

Quingshan and Liang began leaving the beach earlier each evening in hopes of catching more fish, but the best hours of good fishing at night last only so long. And the fishing was still not good yet, so their efforts to work harder brought only more disappointment.

Quingshan's family tried eating less. But fishermen must have energy to work, and eating less was what had made Jiao ill in the first place. There was just not enough money, food, or energy anymore.

Finally, Quingshan became so discouraged that he decided he would resume working seven days a week. He didn't want to violate the Sabbath hours. He didn't want to desecrate God's holy day, but what else could he do? He was not catching more fish; his wife continued to be ill; and he was still in debt.

Part 5: Faith Restored, Miracle Follows

Quingshan's heart was heavy on Friday as he prepared the skiff for a night of fishing. He could hardly look at Liang as they inspected the nets before folding them and putting them in the boat.

And when the sun settled near the horizon and Quingshan got in the boat to shove off for a night of fishing, Liang refused to go with him.

"But we must go," Quingshan said sadly. "There is no other way. If we are ever to get out of debt, we must work hard."

"No!" Liang said emphatically. "That is not the way to behave as a Seventh-day Adventist Christian. God has asked that we keep His Sabbath holy, and there are no other options. We promised that we would never work again during the hours of the Sabbath, and I plan on keeping that promise."

"Then I will have to go alone," Quingshan replied. "Someone has to provide for the family."

"Please don't do this, Papa," Liang begged. "This is not like you. It's old Satan making you talk this way."

Quingshan said nothing but stood in the boat, his head bowed in sadness.

"Don't you remember the story of the three Hebrews who would not bow to the golden idol even if they were thrown into the fiery furnace? They obeyed God, even though they knew it might cost them their lives." Liang's eyes were shining, as if an angel of God were lighting up his face.

"And the best part of the story is that they did not get burned up by the fire, even though it was heated up seven times hotter. Jesus Himself walked in the flames with them and saved them for their faithfulness. And they lived many more years to witness for God in that pagan land."

Quingshan still said nothing.

"Why don't you come with me to the meeting, Papa?" Liang pleaded. "If you come and pray about this, I know you will feel better. And then after the meeting, if you still feel like you must fish tonight, you can go afterward."

Quingshan hesitated at his son's invitation. He knew what his son was doing, trying to get him to go to church so he would get away from the temptation of going out in his boat. He knew it was a good thing Liang was doing, but it made him ashamed to think that his sixteen-year-old son was being more faithful to God than he.

And, of course, he knew he needed to go to church. He also knew it was dangerous to trifle with the Holy Spirit's calling, lest the devil get inside his heart and weaken him all the more.

And so Quingshan climbed out of the boat and went to church with Liang to welcome the Sabbath and pray with the other believers. He knew going to church would not bring him more money. He did not expect a miracle from God. He did not look for the windows of heaven to open so that golden coins would rain down upon him. But he went anyway, glad for his decision not to go fishing and violate the Sabbath hours.

The next day Quingshan worshiped again with his brothers and sisters and received the approval of Heaven for his efforts to honor God. Pastor Wilbur preached from one of his favorite passages in the Bible; and to Quingshan, it couldn't have been more timely.

" 'I am convinced that neither death nor life, neither angels nor demons, neither the present nor the future, nor any powers, neither height nor depth, nor anything else in all creation, will be able to separate us from the love of God that is in Christ Jesus our Lord' [Romans 8:38, 39, NIV]," the pastor read.

It was a blessed day beyond any Quingshan could recall in recent memory, and all because he had listened to his son and the voice of the Holy Spirit to honor God's holy Sabbath. The power of the Holy Spirit filled his heart now. The sweet gift of peace came over him, and the strength of mind and purpose that had previously been his finally returned. And he now understood the test God had been giving him.

For too many weeks and months, Quingshan had been focusing on the difficulties instead of on the blessings. He had been allowing Satan to discourage him with all of the misfortune that had come into his life.

That was when Quingshan had finally discovered the secret. When a person turns his or her life over to God again and surrenders every discouragement and fear, God will take these distractions and throw them into the bottom of the sea. Then life will be filled with song again, and the heart can serve with even more joy than before.

Quingshan stayed with his church family all day. They worshiped together and ate together and prayed together. During the evening vespers, Pastor Wilbur prayed especially for Quingshan and his faith, asking God to give him a miracle catch. "God, You can do anything," Pastor Wilbur said earnestly, "and we claim Your promises now."

When the Sabbath day was over, Quingshan felt refreshed and truly ready to go out on the sea for another night of fishing.

Liang went with him, and the two of them had the best time a father and son could hope for. They were one again in purpose. As the soft ocean breezes blew in from the south, a new bond had formed between the father and son that would keep them faithful to God for the rest of their lives. No adversity could fracture it; no trial destroy it; no hardship wrestle it from their grip.

And then the blessing Quingshan had prayed for so long was given him. That night a miracle occurred as Quingshan and Liang let down their nets. They caught so many fish that they had to call nearby boats to help them haul in the catch. The nets bulged with so many fish that they feared the nets would break.

But more wonderful for Quingshan and his family than the huge catch was the wonderful testimony in the life of a man who had finally and fully trusted God to provide for his every need.

Summaries of the stories in this book can be found in several early twentieth-century sources. *Our Story of Missions* by William A. Spicer contains reports of most of the stories, and a few are included in *Light Bearers* by Richard W. Schwarz and Floyd Greenleaf. Periodicals such as *The Missionary Leader, Review and Herald, Signs of the Times®*, and *The Youth's Instructor* also mention a number of these miraculous circumstances that God used to spread the three angels' messages.